MW01487372

Taming the Dragon Within

How to Be the Mother-in-Law You've Always Wanted

Leanne Braddock
Ileene Huffard
Zannette A. Uriell

Table of Contents

Acknowledgements

A project like a book never gets off the ground without a willing and able ground crew. Our heartfelt thanks to:

- The 1000+ men and women who answered our online survey and offered their insights and wisdom through their stories and comments. Thank you for sharing such personal parts of your lives and for taking the time to tell us about yourselves. We learned so much from you. You made this effort possible.
- Dr. Bill Flatt and Dr. Ed Gray at Harding University Graduate School of Religion who encouraged, guided, and mentored us in this effort on every step of the journey from inception to finale.
- Ty Jones at Blue Chip Image, for the beautiful design and for his creativity, energy, and patience, especially with all the edits that doing a "book by committee" entails.
- Mark Uriell for sharing his graphics and printing expertise, and Rhonda Gray for the photos.
- Nedra Sparks, Tammie Hacker, Suzannah Foster, and Laura Campbell for all their speed reading and for making this book better than we could have done by ourselves. Any grammatical or typographical errors cannot be attributed to them.

- Leanne's mother Frances Bruce; you know why we're thanking you.
- Sudie and Frank Colvett for sharing their mountain cabin, a beautiful and quiet place to write the first draft.

Others who helped at various waypoints with decisions or just a well-placed word include: Peggy Frazier, Kim and Keith Fussell, Mark and Karen Summers, Tim and Tammie Hacker, Curt and Nedra Sparks, Randy and Brenda Frederick, Mary Lynn Summers, Beverly Acker, Cyndy Fahnestock, Joel Goodman, Lynn and Augustine Tawiah, Mary Claire Watts, Genell Holloway, Denise Henson, Vana Dawidow, Faydra Foster, Patricia Casey, Corinne Graham, Susie Hite, Lisa Hickman, Sharon Shappard, Jane Maness, Brenda Collier, Erin Lewis, Anita Ray, Vickie Medley, Aletha Hardwick, and many others.

And finally, a special thanks to our fabulous, understanding and supportive families. To our husbands, Ed Cookenham, Evertt Huffard, and Mark Uriell, thanks for all the dinners made (or brought home), errands run, hours of listening to our steady streams of ideas, offering words of encouragement, and all the rest. You are our heroes. And to our children, children-in-law, grandchildren, parents and parents-in-law, thanks for inspiring us. We love you.

Leanne Braddock
Ileene Huffard
Zannette Uriell

Introduction

When I first became a mother-in-law in 1992, I was at a loss for how I was supposed to act. In the early years of motherhood, I probably relied more on raising my children the way I was raised (even though when I was a teenager I said I would not let that happen). I mean, other than a few acquired quirks, I didn't turn out all that bad, and so using my own parents as role models and talking with other mothers about what worked for them over the years supplied most of my guidance.

But being a mother-in-law? My own marriage had ended in divorce and neither my parents nor my former in-laws could actively guide me through those waters. So that's when I started searching for a book to help with the task. Not that I had been a "book mother" (reading all the latest books about how to raise children before I lifted a finger, etc), but I thought a good book or two might help, so I went to the library and the bookstores. There I found books on "Raising Baby," "The Toddler Years," Helping Your Child as He/She Enters the World of School," "How to Talk with Your Teenager," and even a few on "Letting Go" as your child leaves for college. But how to be a mother-in-law? Nada, nothing, zilch. So I winged it.

I've always been pretty good at thinking on my feet (24 years as a Naval Officer taught me some of that), so I just treated my son-in-law like I did my daughter and son. Makes sense, right? But after arguing over some hot button topics with my son-in-law during most of my daughter and son-in-law's first Christmas visit, I decided I didn't want to do that anymore, and so I made a deal with myself: I would work hard to keep my mouth shut unless it was a matter of great importance to their health or well-being and I would try to get to know this young man better who instantly became part of my family system. I have watched him through the birth of my three grandchildren and he is a loving and attentive husband and father. I have grown to know him and in the process I have grown to love and respect him.

When I became a mother-in-law again in 2003, this time to a daughter-in-law, I went on the search again for reading material, and I found some books, many of which are listed in the bibliography section of Appendix A, and many offer good to excellent advice. But what seemed to be missing was hearing from actual mothers-in-law and children-in-law about what made their relationships work well, and what actions or situations created cracks or even chasms in their feelings towards each other.

That's when I asked my good friends Ileene Huffard and Zannette Uriell to join me in this journey of discovery. What we have learned from website contributions (http://www.goodmotherinlaw.com) and survey responses (included as Appendix A) during the past four years is shared with you in this book; while it can be summed up with the list of 11 traits included in Appendix B, this list doesn't capture all that we learned. The vast majority of women we encountered do NOT want to be the mother-in-law of joke, song, and myth, but many of them are struggling and don't know how to avoid the pitfalls. They want to "tame the dragon within" (the *Mommy overdrive*) and learn to form strong and loving yet respectful and empowering relationships, with their adult children and children-in-law.

If you are a mother-in-law, prospective mother-in-law, friend of a mother-in-law, or just want an interesting read, this book's for you. Enjoy!

Leanne Braddock

- 1 -

Family Dynamics 101: A Family Factor Primer

Why begin a book about mothers-in-law with a chapter about family dynamics? Because that's where it all begins. Your parents, grandparents, and siblings all contributed either positively or negatively into making you, well, *you*. In turn, you have influenced your spouse and children.

What we learned in our research for this book is that both individual traits and family dynamics contribute to what your "mother-in-law default"

1

setting will be. For many, that "mother-in-law default" works just fine. If you are one of those lucky few who have all the traits and tools you need to be a great mother-in-law, quite frankly, you do not need to read this book. So stop reading right now and give it to someone who does need it.

However, if you think your "mother-in-law default" needs some manual adjustment, you may want to learn what experts say about personality and family dynamics, and hear what we have learned from the survey and website comments of over 1,000 mothers-in-law and children-in-law. If you are looking to be a good mother-in-law, or an even better mother-in-law, please keep reading. We would love to have you join us on this journey.

The family stew

It's the nature of all families to be different. Even what we refer to as a "family" can hold different meanings for different people. For many, it means Mom, Dad, and the kids; for others, it means a single mom and her children; for a growing number, it means grandparents caring for grandchildren; for a minority, it means living with other family members or in temporary care.

Because we are unique individuals with unique experiences, cultural influences, genetic make-up, even differing personalities and temperaments, we all bring distinctive ingredients to that stew we call "family." As that family stew "slow cooks" over a lifespan, these different ingredients, coupled with the different spices that are added (experiences, places, people, and situations), all create family patterns or interactions that are also unique to that family. And so, by their very nature, no two families can be exactly alike. That, in itself, makes the "joining" of families through marriage an even more interesting pot (or some would say "potluck"), and all of this can affect the way you operate as a mother-in-law.

Cartoon copyrighted by Mark Parisi, printed with permission.

Personality

One area of "uniqueness" that flavors the family stew is that of individual temperament and personality. It appears we may inherit tendencies such as being outgoing or wary (extroversion and introversion), the degree of openness to new experiences, emotionality, activity, and agreeableness, just to name a few.[i] Those of us who have been closely acquainted with babies have seen personality tendencies emerging from quite an early age. Consider the newborn who is happy in the arms of whoever is holding him at the time, compared with the baby who cries if anyone even looks her way. How many of us have mothered a first baby who could entertain herself happily for hours from the time she was born, only to have a second child who demanded our every waking moment (or vice versa)? In our research, the issue of being extroverted or introverted, for example, may greatly influence that all important "first impression," when the connection between the mother-in-law and child-in-law is formed in those first few minutes of meeting.

The environment

But certainly we cannot rule out the vast influence of our environment. We inherit tendencies, but those do not destine us to certain outcomes. How many of us have seen a person who flounders in one environment flourish in another?

Environmental factors that may influence us include the geographical setting of our home; historical setting, including "defining moments" such as Pearl Harbor or 9/11; wartime or peacetime; our socioeconomic status; personality traits of our own family members; closeness to extended family and their influences; ethnicity and cultural influences; the effects of prejudice; and many more.

The jury is still out on which factor, nature or nurture, has the greater ultimate influence or even if their influence is equal. However, the first and most influential environment for any person is his or her immediate family and so it is to the family we now turn our attention.

A family is not a static object but rather is an ever-changing system. From the time a couple marries, that "family unit" begins changing. Dorothy S. Becvar and Raphael J. Becvar discuss the "family life cycle"[ii], which includes many predictable changes, with the birth of the first child marking the first major family change, for both parents and child. One significant environmental element that shapes a person may be his or her birth order, a phenomenon that can affect individual traits, family interaction patterns, and life career choices.

Kevin Leman, in *The New Birth Order Book*, discusses how children born to the same biological parents can be so different. A first-born child enters a world of adults where she is the sole focus of her parents' attention. When "the child" needs or wants something, there are always one or two adults around to satisfy that need or want. No vying for attention, nor for the last chicken leg, nor worrying about getting new jeans instead of hand-me-downs.

Leman says that first-borns (and only children), *generally* "tend to be conscientious, well organized, serious, goal-oriented, achieving, people pleasers, and believers in authority."[iii] And bossy. First-borns and only children tend to be "movers and shakers" as adults and are over-represented in upper level management in business (CEOs such as Donald Trump and Bill Gates) and government (Winston Churchill, Saddam Hussein, Josef Stalin, Bill Clinton and George W. Bush are all first-borns). In fact, half of all U.S. presidents and all U.S. astronauts have been the eldest child or the first-born son in the family.[iv]

Second and subsequent children are born into a family where the first-born has already set the stage of what it means to be a child. They encounter a world comprised of both adults and children, and must compete with the older sibling(s) for attention, toys, privileges, and praise. Leman says the second born looks to the first born as a role model and studies what he sees, but then, developing a style of his own, often is completely different.[v] The middle child can tend to get "lost" in the family mix, while the "baby" is often catered to and can become the "clown" of the family. Not surprisingly then, comedians Billy Crystal, Drew Carey, and Steve Martin are all the youngest in their families. So we see that even the same family can produce widely differing offspring. Add to that the complexities of blending birth-order in stepfamilies, and the possibilities grow exponentially.

How does this affect mother-in-law/children-in-law relationships? If both are first-borns, they may face power struggles, while a first-born and a youngest may face over-responsible/under-responsible issues.

Boundaries and such

As the family navigates the predictable events of the family life cycle stages, it must also renegotiate family "boundaries" as influences from the environment (sources outside the family) increase. Unpredictable events, such as an untimely death in the family, teen pregnancy, unemployment, etc., can also create the necessity for families to make changes in structure and boundaries. We have dedicated an entire chapter to the issue of boundaries specifically related to parents and adult children, but since those boundary issues have their seeds in our families of origin, we'll spend a few minutes here on some basics.

A healthy family model consists of at least two well-defined subsystems: Mom and Dad or other primary caregivers (the "executive" subsystem) and the "sibling" or "child" subsystem. [vi] The job of the executive subsystem includes determining and enforcing family rules and ensuring all family members receive adequate care including the basic necessities, love and nurturing, and equitable treatment.

A family works best when these two sub-systems or parts remain distinct. Problems can arise if a child is pulled into the executive subsystem by a parent. This often occurs when the marital relationship is weak and one of the parents uses the child to fulfill his or her emotional needs by taking the child into the role of "confidante." If this happens, it can be much more difficult for the parent to "let go" of the child to another adult relationship when he or she gets married. This "holding on" seems to form the basis of mother-in-law/child-in-law conflict, most often between the mother-in-law and the daughter-in-law.

Closely related is the issue of external boundaries between the family unit and the rest of the world. All families are members (or subsystems) of several different larger "systems." These include the family's neighborhood, their faith community, the school system, their work environment, their clubs or hobby groups, etc. Thus, the "line" the family draws (consciously or unconsciously) between itself and the influence of these other systems is the external family boundary. These external boundaries determine how closed or open the family system is to the influence of other people, situations, and experiences.

So how open or closed should a family's boundaries be? There is no hard and fast rule. A system needs to be open enough to allow room for change and growth, but closed enough to maintain family integrity. If the family is too closed, members will not be able to grow and fulfill their human potential. If it is too open, the family environment will be chaotic and perhaps even open to dangerous influences.[vii]

Also, different circumstances may, at different times, dictate a more open or closed boundary to the family system. As a family moves through its family life cycle it will most likely need to become more open so the children gain the skills and experiences they need to prepare them for the outside world and for forming a healthy family of their own.

How is this all relevant?

So what does this have to do with being a mother-in-law? If you have read this far, you have probably figured it out by now. Becoming a mother-in-law requires boundary negotiations as you:

1) accept another person into your family system and

2) learn to release your child to his or her spouse so they can form their own unique family. Unfortunately, like most of the other "stage critical tasks" in the family life cycle, that's easier said than done.

Regrettably, mothers-in-law have some things going against them: prejudices, bad jokes, terrible stories, and at least one disgusting song. There exists a cultural bias against mothers-in-law in our American society. Sadly, some of it is deserved.

In response to the open-ended questions on the survey and website, we heard about mothers-in-law who lied about their child-in-law to the rest of the family, criticized their child-in-law at nearly every opportunity, and even a few who are credited with making sure the marriage ended. We have heard of others who don't respect the boundaries of their children's marriages and want their grown children to put their mother's needs above those of their spouse's, and many, many more. There are some in-laws who are just plain toxic.[viii]

But we also heard stories of wonderful mothers-in-law who showed amazing sensitivity and love towards their children-in-law in ways that made us weep; of close in-law relationships that have spanned six decades; and remarkable stories of forgiveness and reconciliation.

After all is said and done, the aim of this book is to help those women who don't want to be the mothers-in-law of joke, story, and song successfully navigate this family change and become the mothers-in-law they themselves would want to have. We'll start at "The Beginning".

---

[i] Duane P. Schultz and Sydney Ellen Schultz, *Theories of Personality* (Belmont, CA: Wadsworth, 2001), 476-77.
[ii] Dorothy S. Becvar and Raphael J. Becvar, *Family Therapy: A Systemic Integration* (Needham Heights, MA: Allyn and Bacon, 2000), 137.
[iii] Kevin Leman, *The New Birth Order Book* (Grand Rapids: Baker Book, 1998), 78.

[iv] BBC News of 2 Sept 2003,
http://news.bbc.co.uk/2/hi/talking_point/3187841.stm accessed 9
June 2006.
[v] Leman, 151.
[vi] Salvador Minuchin, *Families and Family Therapy*
(Cambridge, MA: Harvard Press, 1974), 51-53.
[vii] Becvar and Becvar, 23.
[viii] Susan Forward, *Toxic In-Laws* (New York: Quill, 2002).

- 2 -

Beginnings:
Why First Meetings
Are Important

Chances are that when you first realized you were going to be a mother-in-law, you were flooded with many thoughts and emotions, some of them good and some of them, maybe, not so good.

I (Leanne) was stationed in Iceland with the Navy when my daughter called from college in Arkansas to tell me she and her boyfriend had decided to marry. I remember thinking, "She's so young," then "I'm not old enough yet to be a mother-in-law (I'm only 40)," and then "I haven't even met this person!" That's the thing about in-laws: they are relative strangers (except to your adult child), but in the flash of a wedding photographer's bulb, they become, well, relatives.

We spend 18, 20, 30 years getting to know our child, but usually only have a fraction of that time to get to know our future in-laws. No wonder first meetings can be so highly stressful for both mothers-in-law and the children-in-law, particularly daughters-in-law. Even if the couple has dated for a few years, the "first meeting" can be the one after it dawns on the child-in-law and the mother-in-law that marriage is in the offing. Both mother-in-law and child-in-law question, "What if they don't like me?" "What if I don't meet her/his expectations?" "How much of me will I have to change to be part of this family (or to make room for this person in my family)?" Whether we admit it or not, when we realize we may be looking at our future child-in-law, we begin sizing them up, picturing him or her at family gatherings, and imagining who all will be at the house after the birth of their first child.

Many factors can filter your first meeting and subsequent relationship with your future child-in-law. Does this person meet the expectations you had for a child-in-law? Are you alike or different personality-wise? Are you from the same religious or cultural background? Is the couple quite young? Is he or she from "the other side of the tracks"? Or the other side of the country? Has the future child-in-law been married before? Is your child the last fledgling to leave the nest? Let's take a look at a few of these factors.

From www.CartoonStock.com, used with permission.

First, Leanne's not-so-stellar approach

My daughter had just celebrated her 19th birthday when she called to tell me she and my future son-in-law planned to marry the following summer, and I was terrified she was making a big mistake because of my own failed early marriage. Not long after she called, I flew to Arkansas (from

Iceland!) and tried to talk both my daughter and my future son-in-law into postponing the wedding for 2 years until they finished school. That was the first time I had met my future son-in-law. (Really classy approach, huh?) They stood firm and I flew home to Iceland to finish out my tour there.

A few months before the wedding, I transferred to Washington, DC, where I went to see a therapist hoping that he could help me figure out a way to convince my daughter not to marry so young. He listened for 45 minutes to my non-stop blathering. When I finally stopped and took a deep breath and asked him what I should do, he gave me some of the best advice I've ever received. He told me to enjoy the time I had with my daughter for the month she would be home before the wedding. He asked what fun things we liked to do together, and then he told me to go do them. "That way," he said, "if all those problems come to pass, you will have continued to build a relationship with her and she will feel free to come and talk with you." He was also telling me that my daughter was an adult and I needed to respect her wishes. That sentiment was echoed by one mother-in-law:

"The life choices that our children make for themselves may not be a choice you would make for

them. You don't have to love the person that your son or daughter marries, but you have to accept it or ultimately cause emotional hurt for your child."

This boils down to "The bird is leaving the nest to make his own. Wish him well." Now, 14 years later, I can't imagine our family without my son-in-law and I love him like a son.

A word about expectations

The question isn't whether or not you want to have a relationship with your child-in-law; at issue is what **kind** of relationship you want to have. By reading this book, we believe you want to have a good relationship, so a couple of important basic principles come into play here.

No matter what you imagined your child's future spouse would look like, act like, how educated you expected him or her to be, what he or she would do for a living, or any other facet you had envisioned, none of that imagining has a place here. Reality rules. You cannot change another person. You might be able to influence another person but you cannot change them. If (after meeting your future child-in-law) changing him or her is what you have in mind, forget it, it won't work.

You can change yourself, including changing your expectations. It might take some time, it might take letting go of some long-held beliefs, but it can be done, and, in the end, will probably bode better for the relationship. We know this might be hard truth, but please read on.

From www.CartoonStock.com, used with permission.

Personality differences

Everybody has a personality, and oh, can they be different. Probably one of the most obvious personality differences is the extrovert/introvert factor. Of course, people can fall anywhere along the spectrum, but classification of each lies in where they recharge and gain energy. Extroverts get their energy from being with and around other people. They are generally outgoing, have a lot of acquaintances, and often talk a lot. Too much solitary time drives them right out the door, so they can bask in the middle of the humanity stew.

Introverts, on the other hand, recharge their batteries by being alone and having quiet time to think and ponder, and they generally think more deeply about issues than extroverts. They have friends, but are often more selective and remain close to only a handful of people. Introverts aren't hermits, and many enjoy careers as successful public speakers. But too much racket, activity, or people can wear them out and deplete their energy. Current research in brain mapping even shows that introverts and extroverts process information differently and have different dominant brain chemicals.[i]

However, if your future child-in-law is an introvert and you are an extrovert, you may perceive her quietness and choosing to take a few moments by herself as not liking or appreciating you. If you require her presence at all activities, she may classify you as bossy or overbearing. On the other hand, an introvert mother-in-law may find it difficult to connect with an outgoing, gregarious, future child-in-law and could even feel a bit intimidated by all that energy. You both want to do the right thing, but you have different personalities and different ways of interacting.

My daughter-in-law is an introvert, and while we are vastly different in that aspect, I have learned to appreciate her astute observation of people and situations as well as her need to have some alone time when she visits. But early in our relationship, when she was visiting, I was puzzled at why she would go to the guest room and read for an hour or so during the day. I would ask my son (and eventually her), "Did I do something wrong? Did I offend in some way?" Now I understand that our family of (primarily) extroverts simply wears her out, and she needs some time alone to recharge her batteries before joining in our activities again.

It's important for extroverts to realize that being an introvert is a personality trait and not a character disorder. Until I learned more about introverts, I think I assumed that introverts were just shy extroverts waiting for someone to pull them out of their shells, not fully engaged people in their own way.

Religious and cultural differences

Differences (or perceived differences) in religion and culture can color your view of a future child-in-law and vice versa. One young American woman described her experiences dating a man from Tbilisi, Georgia (in the former Soviet Union). Evidently there, "girlfriends are seen as in-laws in the making – and are scrutinized accordingly," from advice against coffee drinking (bad for childbearing) to "turn of the century marriage advice."[ii] And that occurred within just a few weeks of meeting his mother!

As a future mother-in-law of a child-in-law from a different culture, probably the best stance to take is one of getting to know more about her as a person and how she views her cultural influence. To assume that because you have a Hispanic friend, your Hispanic future daughter-in-law is just like her, would be a mistake. That's like saying all Americans are alike.

While there are some general similarities within cultures, each individual is different and the cultural backgrounds influence him or her in individual ways. It may be a sharper learning curve for both of you, but approach your relationship as a work in progress and stay as open-minded as you can. We've included more information about cultural differences in a later chapter, which may help you start off on the right foot.

Religious differences can be quite emotional because that cuts to the core of who we are and what we believe. Again, taking a stance of interest and understanding is the best approach. One of the survey respondents said she respected her mother-in-law for accepting her and her husband's religious choices even though there was pressure at first for her to accept his religion.

Prior marriages

Sometimes a child's or future child-in-law's prior marriages or relationships can affect the lens with which a mother-in-law views her prospective child-in-law. In a later chapter, we discuss divorce and the mother-in-law in greater detail, but a mother-in-law's "hesitant" approach to the new child-in-law, even if it's based on fear of being hurt again or being ashamed, can communicate non-acceptance to the new child-in-law. That happened in this case:

"[My mother-in-law] is, at times, hesitant with me because of my husband's prior failed marriage. For example, she only bought pictures of our wedding with her family in them. I wasn't in any of them. It definitely hurt my feelings, but I'm not even sure she realized what she was doing."

But not all mothers-in-law react that way. Here is a heart-warming example we received about an exceptional mother-in-law:

"I am engaged to be married. No date has been set. But I have a great relationship with my future mother-in-law. I already call her my Mother-in-Law and vice versa. She is like a friend. I can go to her about anything. She has taken up with my daughter from a previous marriage. She loves the idea of being a grandma. She is there when I need her. We all have a good time when we are together. We have respect for each other. We have not had the first cross word towards each other and I have known her for two years now. She welcomes me and my daughter to her family and makes us feel loved and a part of the family."

Dysfunctional families

Sometimes, dysfunctional family patterns can create problems in early mother-in-law/child-in-law relationships. If a mother expects her adult child to be her primary emotional support, she often views the new spouse as competition for her adult child's affection and does not respect the new primary relationship her child has formed with the new spouse. Drawing from biblical wording, your adult child is to "leave his/her parents and cleave to his/her mate." Leaving and cleaving become far more difficult to do when a parent is holding onto the adult child. One of the mothers-in-law put it this way:

> *"Accept that children are not in romantic relationships with parents but have to grow up and live their own lives. When parents understand this then we all will be better off."*

Survey says...

Interestingly, our research indicates that mothers-in-law and children-in-law who immediately liked one another have continued a good relationship after the wedding. So what does that tell us we need to do? Just like one another immediately and we'll have a great relationship?

That's easier said than done, and of course, it's a bit more complex than that because relationships are dynamic. But making a good start seems to be important. As the old adage goes, "You never get a second chance to make a good first impression," so be ready.

In the last chapter, we touched on family boundaries. If yours have been a bit rigid, now is the time to expand them. Chances are that the older your children get, the more likely they are to find someone they want to marry and bring into the family system. Parents who start cultivating a welcoming attitude when their children begin dating may have an easier time assimilating other people into their families. A friend of mine told me that, beginning when her only son was in high school, she started treating every date he brought home as the woman he may eventually marry (and who, she said, might be the one to select her nursing home one day!). She claims it helped teach her to accept others for who they are and, by the time her son did bring home "the one," she was much better able to welcome her into the family.

The survey respondents often mentioned early warmth and acceptance as something they most value in their mothers-in-law:

"She accepted me for who I was and appreciated my uniqueness."

"She accepted me from the beginning and always took my side."

"She accepted me from the beginning and trusted her son's judgment in marrying me."

"She accepted me as a daughter."

"She welcomed me into the family with open arms."

"She supported our desire to be married and also accepted me into the family as I had been previously married with a child."

"From the beginning she made me feel welcome in her home and with the family, she made me feel wanted and valued."

And this advice from both mothers-in-law and children-in-law:

"You need to start out on the right foot, get to know each other, accept each other, and respect them 100%."

"Accept the differences between people. Don't expect the perfect relationship that you may see in others, but deal with your unique relationship."

"Accept each other as you are; bring out the best in each other."

"If each would go into the relationship without being judgmental and with no unfair expectations, it would be easier to accept each other at face value. Realize you both love the same person and want what is best for that person."

Seek first to understand

Accepting someone is one thing, but as Albert Ellis once said, "Acceptance is not love," so if you aspire to a deeper relationship with your child-in-law, you need to take another step. In Stephen Covey's bestseller, *The Seven Habits of Highly Effective People*, the fifth habit states, "Seek first to understand, then to be understood."[iii] Covey explains that if a person seeks to interact effectively with another, she must first understand that person.

This can be accomplished by means of empathic listening.

While a later chapter deals in more depth with communication issues, it's worth noting here that most people do not really listen to one another. Rather, we listen with what Covey calls "the intent to reply." In other words, we are looking for elements in what the other person is saying so we can formulate an intelligent and often persuasive reply.

When we do that, we are not truly listening to what the speaker is telling us. Empathic listening involves active listening and often rephrasing what was said in an effort to fully understand the message. The key, Covey says, to empathic listening is having the best interest of the other person at heart. When we seek to better understand another person rather than engage in conversation aimed at "being understood" ourselves, we model caring and "valuing" and set the stage for deeper relationships.

Most experts agree that the mother-in-law, as the older and (hopefully) wiser individual, should take the lead in setting the tone and modeling behavior for the relationship.[iv] The survey findings indicate that mothers-in-law feel more self-assured and "comfortable in their own skin" so to speak, and it makes sense they would be the ones to take the lead. Generally, all it takes at an initial meeting or marriage-intent announcement is for the mother-in-law to offer an embrace, a few welcoming words, an approving smile, or a warm handshake.[v] But some stories we received talked about much more that their mother-in-law had done. Here's one:

> *"My mother-in-law had 3 sons. I was the first daughter-in-law. When we became engaged, I was already 36 years old and a little uncertain about the whole "traditional bride" thing. She sent me a subscription to a bridal magazine! When we actually found a gown that we both loved in one of the magazines, she was over the moon! The next time we visited, she asked if she might go gown shopping with us. She was priceless! It was like playing dress up, only with me as the doll. She then took us to lunch and wept as she talked about how much her mother would have loved me. When we got home, she spoke with my mom over the phone and told her how beautiful I was."*

Clearly this daughter-in-law felt accepted, welcomed, and embraced by her future mother-in-law.

Permission to marry

In this modern era, asking for permission to marry appears antiquated at best, however parental approval continues to exert powerful influence. In their book *The Blessing*, Gary Smalley and John Trent state that parental approval can impact us even if we are not currently on speaking terms with our parents, and that the relationship that we have with our parents can affect all our other relationships (current as well as future).[vi] Offering your child and child-in-law your blessing doesn't mean that you agree with everything, but it may set the stage for a close family relationship.

Honoring one another

Gary Smalley uses the idea of "honor" to describe the key ingredient of a loving and lasting marriage relationship. Honor is defined as attaching "high value, worth, or importance to a person or thing," and Smalley believes that choosing to honor our spouses can positively transform any marriage.[vii]

When I'm doing family therapy, I often ask family members to name someone they greatly admire or honor. Some people name ministers, teachers, sports figures, entertainers, etc., after which I ask them, "If that person came to your house for dinner or a visit, how would you treat him or her? Where would you let them sit? How would you act around them?" Usually they tell me they would be respectful, not swear, not yell at the "honoree," and allow him to sit anywhere he would like to sit. Then I ask, "What would happen if that's how you treated your family members?"

Gloria Horsley, in her book *The In-Law Survival Guide,* also reflects this theme and suggests parents ask themselves if they are respecting their child's friend as they would a future child-in-law. And for children to ask themselves if they are treating their friend/partner's parents as they would future in-laws.[viii] Implementing respect and honor for one another can go a long way in relationship building with your future child-in-law.

Need a "do over"?

What if you have blown the first meeting with your child-in-law and now you want to salvage it? My advice: apologize, ask for a "do over," and move smartly forward on the right foot. While apologizing requires a bit of humility and transparent-ness, it remains the surest way to clear the path for forgiveness among businesses, governments, and interpersonal relationships.[ix] When we asked the children-in-law respondents what single small thing would have the most positive effect on their relationship with their mothers-in-law, over half said, "Apologize."

"Apologize for past wrongs."

"Apologize for making fun of me at a family gathering when we were dating."

Making the best of a difficult situation

Sometimes, even after you do your very best, the initial relationship between mother-in-law and child-in-law remains difficult. We have dozens of stories from both mothers-in-law and children-in-law who tell of in-laws who, from one perspective, deliberately tried to sabotage either the mother-in-law/adult child relationship or the adult child/child-in-law relationship, usually with heart-breaking results. Here's one example from a mother-in-law:

"My story is much too involved and long to leave here. In a nutshell, I deal with the daughter-in-law from hell. She completely banished me from her and my son's lives even before the wedding. They have 3 children I'm not allowed to see. Two boys who I only saw at birth and a girl I've never seen, nor will I ever be allowed to see. I've done

everything I know to do to cultivate a relationship with this woman, to no avail."

And from a daughter-in-law:

"My mother-in-law had an outwardly pleasant demeanor, with a subtext of competition and hostility she only showed when her son was not around. She once told me angrily that before I came along SHE was the most important woman in her son's life (when I came along he was 32)... My husband never emotionally broke from his birth family and when people ask about his family I note he starts to talk about them before us. His siblings hate me now because of his mother's constant harping against me, and the effect on our marriage has been devastating and probably fatal."

What do you do?   My good friend and colleague, Dr. Bill Flatt, says, "You can't [let yourself] feel bad about doing the right thing." The right thing to do in the early stages of the relationship usually means, "Keep trying." Take the high road, model love and forgiveness, and continue trying to open up communication and to keep the possibility of a relationship alive.   Now, do you have a wedding ahead? If so, turn the page.

[i] Marti Olsen Laney, *The Introvert Advantage* (New York: Workman Publishing, 2002), 71-75.

[ii] Julie Guyot, "Mother-in-Laws: The threat is closer than you think," http://www.bootsnall.com/travelstories/asia/may03mother.sht ml accessed on 21 June 2006.

[iii] Stephen Covey, *The Seven Habits of Highly Effective People* (New York: Simon & Schuster, 1989).

[iv] Annie Chapman, *The Mother-in-Law Dance* (Eugene, OR: Harvest House, 2004), 27-39.

[v] Helene S. Arnstein, *Between Mothers-in-Law and Daughters-in-Law* (New York: Dodd, Mead & Co., 1985), 11.

[vi] Gary Smalley and John Trent, *The Blessing* (New York: Pocket Books, 1986), 11.

[vii] Gary Smalley, *Hidden Keys of a Loving, Lasting Marriage* (Grand Rapids, MI: Zondervan, 1984), 41.

[viii] Gloria Call Horsley, *The In-Law Survival Guide* (New York: John Wiley & Sons, 1997), 64.

[ix] Howard Kushner, "The Power of Apology: Removing the Legal Barriers," Special Report No. 27 to the Legislative Assembly of British Columbia (Feb 2006); Seiji Takaku, "The Effects of Apology and Perspective Taking on Interpersonal Forgiveness: A Dissonance-Attribution Model of Interpersonal Forgiveness," *Journal of Social Psychology* 141, no. 4 (Aug 2001), p. 494-508.

- 3 -

The Wedding (War or Peace?)

If anyone doubts the solvency of the wedding industry, take a look at these figures. The average cost of a wedding in the United States today hovers around $27,000, not including the cost of the honeymoon, the engagement ring, and a bridal consultant or a wedding planner. If you live in Memphis, Tennessee, that amount increases to almost $33,000; in the Washington, DC area, the cost creeps to over $56,000; and if you live in beautiful Malibu, California, the average there spikes to a whopping $109,000![i] Fortunately, many people get by on much less, but a wedding still represents one of the major investments a family makes.

Realizing the monetary, time, and emotional investment that goes into that special day, probably one of the first discussions you need to have with your adult child and future child-in-law is to find out what beliefs and expectations **they** hold about the wedding and how **they** see your role and responsibilities. (We'll talk about who pays a little later in this chapter.)

In modern Western society, popular wedding etiquette dictates this is the "Day for the Bride." Almost every popular bridal magazine, chat forum, and wedding planning book exhorts the bride, "This is YOUR day. Do what YOU want to do!" That might sell a lot of products, but, like much of the popular advice so readily available, it needs a reality check.

Weddings have long represented not just a uniting of two people, but a joining of families and sometimes even communities, tribes, and nations. While your adult child's wedding may not influence world affairs, chances are that it may influence family affairs for years to come, and so holds a place of high importance.

When we asked survey participants, only 23% of the daughters-in-law said they had conflict with their future mother-in-law over wedding plans, but those that reported conflict were also less likely to enjoy a current good relationship with their mother-in-law. Forty-six percent of the daughters-in-law stated they invited their future mother-in-law's participation in the wedding, and those who did were more likely to currently enjoy a good relationship with their mothers-in-law.

Let me note here that the couple may not want to involve family at all in the wedding itself, and instead they may choose to elope or go off to some isolated place, find two witnesses and a minister along the way, and tie the knot. In fact, that's exactly what two friends of mine did.

When Beverly and Terry got married, they went to one of the most beautiful spots in the country, the banks of the Snake River. They wrote their own vows and celebrated that day in a way that was totally unique and meaningful for just the two of them. They called ahead and lined up a judge in town to marry them. He told them, "Your job is to show up and mine is to find the witnesses."

The next afternoon Beverly, carrying the yellow roses her mother had wired to her, drove through the brisk air to a parking area where they met the judge. Terry, a professional photographer, had lined up a local photographer to record the wedding. She was waiting for them, so the judge went on a search for one more witness. He found a man snapping pictures on a beaver pond and asked him to serve as the second witness. He agreed on the condition they let him take pictures of the wedding too. Two witnesses and both photographers to boot! Beverly said when the ceremony was over she looked around and both photographers were crying. That worked for Beverly and Terry, and both families understood and blessed the ceremony they chose.

Here's another story from a respondent:

"[My mother-in-law] is the type of person who would have probably loved a big wedding and all the trappings that go with it. But because of my family situation, after 6 months of being engaged, we felt eloping was the right choice. My mother-in-law is the only person we told before we eloped. She was initially shocked, and wanted to talk to us and make sure we had really thought it through, etc. Once she understood where we were coming from, she was immediately supportive. We told her our decision on a Monday afternoon, and our plan was to leave town on Tuesday morning to go to Gatlinburg and elope. We went."

However, if the happy couple plans to invite any guests at all, they will have to share the planning of this day with other people, including their parents and in-laws. A few words about expectations seem in order.

Unrealistic expectations? Weddings set the stage for disasters to happen. As with the holidays, the popular media paints an unrealistic picture of what a wedding must be. Movies and wedding magazines, urged on by the wedding consulting business, all portray the upcoming wedding taking place on a perfect sunny day, with perfect attendants, perfect parents and in-laws, a perfect groom, and of course, a perfect bride. In fact, all the bride has to do is to slip into her perfect wedding gown and glide down a red carpet to her beloved.

Does that sound like Cinderella or what? No wonder insurance companies now offer wedding insurance where, for pennies on the dollar, you are protected from financial liability against unforeseen problems on or before the wedding day (one more indication of the expectation for perfection). That's not to say it doesn't happen just that way somewhere, sometime, in some galaxy far, far away. Unfortunately, two things work against such a fantasy: 1) stuff happens and things don't always go as planned, and 2) each person may have a different idea of what "perfect" looks like; both can set the stage for conflicts, hurt feelings, and out and out war.

Women have often been called "kin keepers"[ii] in that they are the ones who most often hold the family together emotionally. They arrange family get-togethers, keep in touch with cards and letters, and remember to send photos to grandmothers. Being "kin keepers," combined with the fact that one woman has spent more time thinking about weddings during her lifetime than 100,000 men all put together, means the wedding plans are often made by the women in the family. Those women usually include the bride, her mother, and perhaps her future mother-in-law. If there are sisters or sisters-in-law, they may also figure prominently, as well as the bride's friends. Whether or not the mother-in-law is actually invited to join in the wedding planning, all the women in the family have been thinking about this day for years, especially the mothers. Even when my (Leanne) children were babies, I remember rocking them and thinking that someday they would be getting married, and I envisioned those weddings just as I had envisioned my own wedding as a little girl. I don't think I'm alone.

The trouble is, all of these women come to the wedding planning table with many years of mental pictures, and not all those mental pictures look alike.

The picture I have been detailing for 20-30 years may clash with those of the other women in this event. The survey found that brides in their thirties reported the greatest conflict with their mothers-in-law over wedding details. Perhaps women in that age bracket had a more completely formed picture of what they wanted their weddings to be and were less likely to accept input.

From www.CartoonStock.com, used with permission.

The bride's mental picture of "a perfect wedding" may include only the immediate family and closest friends, while her future mother-in-law may be thinking it would be a great time for a family reunion when all eight of her siblings and their families could come and enjoy the time together. The mother might have always dreamed of her father, a Baptist minister, performing the wedding ceremony, while her the bride thinks Rabbi Chuck, whom she knows from yoga class, would be the perfect one to administer the vows. The groom, who has probably spent a nanosecond in his entire life thinking about a wedding, is, if anything, thinking about the honeymoon. So what do we do?

The first dance

In their new series, *The First Dance*, father and daughter team William J. Doherty (family therapist) and Elizabeth Doherty Thomas (recent bride), state, "Weddings are life long bonds with new, extended family… Every stage of the planning forges a new family and community, for better or worse."[iii] They suggest the engaged couple approach the wedding planning experience as a first opportunity to work together as a couple as they negotiate with one another and with other family members. "Brides don't lose sleep over floral arrangements," they say, "but over conflicts with their mothers [and mothers-in-law?] about floral arrangements." In other words, it's not the wedding planning that's difficult, but rather dealing with all the family members.[iv] Instead of the motto, "It's my wedding, I'll do what I want," Doherty and Thomas propose the motto, "It's our wedding and you're an important part of it so let's figure it out."[v]

How can a parent help?

The "nearly perfect" wedding?

In her book, *How to Be the Perfect Mother-in-Law*, Camille Russo talks about how pressure on the bride (from both the inside and outside) to have a "perfect" wedding can turn a sweet girl into "the Bride of Frankenstein."[vi] It can make her say and do things she wouldn't be caught dead doing or saying any other time. Striking out at grandmothers and friends, she's a stressed out mess. Russo suggests that rather than being lured into that dungeon by a quest for perfection, the bride at least consider the option of the "nearly perfect wedding." Russo says that things won't ruin a wedding as much as a bride who wants everything to be picture-perfect.

If you are the mother of the bride, help her get things into perspective. The wedding day is one day in her life and you want it to be as special as possible.

But the wedding is not the sum total of her life. The wedding day will come and it will pass in 24 hours. Her family and friends will be there for much longer. Encourage her to develop a plan with her fiancé and maybe have a joint meeting with all the parents to work out details in the spirit of family connectedness. If you are the mother of the groom, have a sit-down talk with your son pronto.

The sit-down talk

First, remember your son has probably avoided weddings (unless he was a best man, and then it was just a party to him) and his level of urgency about wedding preparations lags behind the national debt. I remember talking with my future daughter-in-law about a month before the wedding, and I casually asked, "How are things going?" She told me about all the stuff she had accomplished for the big day and I shared with her some items I had agreed to arrange. That's when she told me she had asked my son six months earlier to do only two things, neither of which he had done and, frankly, she was getting pretty irritated about it (so was I).

Next, discuss with him how important this wedding ceremony is to his betrothed. Seemingly small details may carry with them pieces of her childhood fantasy or a family tradition and must be honored and explored. Even if your son doesn't have a specific "to do" list, let him know the importance of being a participating partner in the discussion when his beloved is talking about the wedding. If she asks him a question about wedding details, such as "Should we have real flowers or silk ones?" tell him his first response should be, "What do you think about that, Honey?" and then either discuss options or, if he agrees or truly has no opinion, agree with her. Never, under any circumstances, should he say, "It doesn't matter." It **does matter** to her, so help him understand it needs to matter to him.

When I've done pre-marital counseling, the groom will sometimes say, "It seems like all we've talked about for the past six months is the wedding!" I have gently urged them to try and confine wedding talk to 30 minutes each day or 2 hours each week, so they can focus on other aspects of their upcoming marriage. If you are the mother of the groom, I would not recommend you try to urge him to do that alone. Maybe you can enlist the help of the mother of the bride. Otherwise, you will all just have to tough it out. That day will come and go, and soon all the wedding preparation talk will be over.

Who's in charge = Who's paying?

The couple getting married should have the kind of wedding celebration they want, but often the decision-making reverts to the one who is footing the bill. Up until about thirty or forty years ago, the bride's family paid for the wedding ceremony and the groom's family paid for the rehearsal dinner, and each had their territory pretty clearly marked.

Today, there are many options. Some families still opt to pay for their son or daughter's wedding completely. Some couples foot the full bill in its entirety. And, perhaps more common now because of the high cost of weddings, the two families and the couple share the costs. All of that makes for some confusing rights and responsibilities, and requires flexibility. Doherty and Thomas call all of those involved in the wedding process (family, friends, both paying and non-paying) "stakeholders." They all have some interest in the wedding plans, and, "They care not only about what was decided, but also about how they were involved in the decision."[vii] Because the territory is not clearly marked, perhaps we need to spend some time discussing the art of conflict resolution.

Handling conflict

Let me introduce you to a concept that a good friend and colleague, Willie Holcomb, uses when counseling couples. It's called the "High Threat"/"Low Threat" concept. And you only have to ask yourself one or two questions to determine your course of action. It is: "Am I in a high threat or a low threat situation?" A high threat situation is one in which there is a strong likelihood you will be killed or seriously injured. If I'm walking out of the grocery store and a man runs up, hits me, and grabs my purse, that's a high threat situation, and I need to react in kind with a high threat response. Yelling and screaming, fighting, and fleeing would all be appropriate responses to a high threat situation.

However, anything less than the threat of death or serious injury is a low threat situation, and requires a low threat response. For example, if I'm in a slow moving check-out line at the same grocery store, and the cashier is carrying on a chit-chat with everyone in front of me, and I've had a really hard day at work so I'm tired and irritable, is that a high threat or a low threat situation? If I want to know the answer, I ask myself, "Am I in immediate danger of death or serious injury?" In this case, the answer is obviously no, so it calls for a low threat response, which might include reminding myself that I am not in control of that situation and that if it takes me a few more minutes to get home, so what? Since patience is not my greatest virtue, a slow-moving line may interfere with what Willie would call my "happiness bubble," but it doesn't call for anger, yelling, rude comments, or any of those higher threat responses.

How does that apply to weddings? If, for example, my son and future daughter-in-law decide to have a small intimate wedding on the top of a mountain where only the fit and hearty can travel (meaning most of our relatives and friends will not be there), I may find myself getting a little upset about that. But, as soon as I realize I'm upset, I ask myself, "Am I in immediate danger of death or serious injury?" The answer is no, so that's a low threat situation requiring a low threat response. Screaming and yelling and threatening not to come to the wedding at all are not appropriate reactions. Asking them if they had thought of the limitations on attendees, asking them if they would consider changing their minds, asking them what I'm supposed to wear to such an event, etc., are all appropriate responses.

Here's another example. Suppose my future daughter-in-law's family gave me the names/numbers of people who were coming to the rehearsal dinner (for which my husband and I are paying), and, at the last minute, half of them cancelled because they decide to go to a tractor pull instead. Frustrating? Yep. Costly? Maybe, if I've already obligated for the food. But am I in immediate danger of death or serious injury? Obviously not. Take the leftover food home and serve it to your husband for the next six weeks.

See how this works? Just try it the next time you feel yourself getting tense or angry about something, and see if it doesn't put things into perspective.

That's not to say that nothing is important except high threat situations. Many things are important. But often in the fabricated high drama of weddings, frustrations are magnified and people say and do things they would not normally do because they are still expecting that illusive "perfect." If your son-in-law's family doesn't hold to the same social standards you do, ignoring or insulting them probably won't change them, but it might change the way your son-in-law feels about you. Take the high road and be gracious. It might make a difference in your future relationship.

The nature of relationships: Forming, storming, norming, and conforming

Hopefully you have gotten to know your child-in-law and his/her family before this event takes place, but if you haven't, or if you haven't known one another very well, knowing a bit about the phases of relationship-building may help. In her book *The In-Law Survival Guide*, Gloria Horsley equates the stages of in-law development to those of other groups: forming, storming, norming, and conforming.[viii]

When groups are "forming," people tend to put their best face forward. They try to get to know one another (as much as their own "filters" allow) and seek commonalities. Only later, when the masks come off, do the problems surface. If you are in this phase of relationship with your child-in-law and his/her family when the wedding preparations take place, you may all be putting your best foot forward and if there are conflicts, they are covered up, ignored, or "stuffed," and may resurface at a later time, such as when the photos come back ("I hated that dress your mother wore at our wedding, but my mother didn't want to hurt her feelings, so we didn't say anything!")

During the "storming" phase, the honeymoon period of the relationship has ended and the real selves, and resulting conflict, come to the fore. Differences of opinion are expressed and alternatives discussed. If you are in the storming phase when making wedding preparations, you will be more open with one another, but you also may have more open conflict. Remember, during this phase it's important to negotiate, calmly and peaceably. If negotiation skills are not employed during this phase, people can get their feelings hurt and a rift that may last for years could develop and inhibit the group from moving to the next phase of development.

During the "norming" phase, groups reach an equilibrium, either coming to a common understanding or agreeing to disagree. They have confronted most conflicts and are able to move forward on decisions. Weddings that are planned during this phase may have less unresolved conflict than those planned in earlier phases because all the players have reached a higher level of comfort with one another. Family members and future in-laws may disagree, but they will probably feel more comfortable discussing the issues.

In the "conforming" stage, cohesion has been reached and rules have been established and agreed upon.[ix] Weddings planned between members who have reached this group phase will be relatively conflict-free or conflict can be resolved more readily.

However, unexpected events, the introduction of new people, and many other elements can affect a group so that its status may need to be renegotiated.

All relationships go through these phases, some more quickly than others, and can vary from months to years depending on how much conflict there is to resolve, how much contact members have with one another, and many other factors.

Interestingly, the daughters-in-law who knew their mothers-in-law between two and three years before the wedding were more likely to report conflict than those who knew their future mother-in-law for more than three years or less than two years. Though the survey didn't ask specifically about group development, the data suggest that perhaps those mothers-in-law and children-in-law who had known each other between two and three years were experiencing the "storming" phase of their relationship and hence experienced greater conflict. This same group also reported a higher instance of their future spouse feeling "caught in the middle." Perhaps being aware of these relationship phases and their characteristics will help you determine where you are and give you a better perspective on any conflict you are still encountering.

Divorced, remarried, and other parent and in-law situations

Below is a list of some of the situations that call for heroic negotiation:

- Your son wants to invite his father (your ex-husband), who wants to bring his new wife (the one he left you for).
- Your future daughter-in-law's parents are going through a divorce and both say they will not attend if the other comes.
- You future son-in-law's father has recently "come out" and wants to bring his partner to the wedding (being held at your very conservative Christian church).

If any of the above situations, or other similarly difficult ones, come to light, allow your adult child and child-in-law the opportunity, with your encouragement and support, to negotiate a settlement between the parties. (Remember, wedding planning is the first training ground for their future negotiation and conflict resolution.) You have a responsibility to express your own feelings and to be sensitive to the feelings of others, but it's helpful here to remember a couple of things. First, remember that weddings are high-stress, short-term events and not life or death situations. (However, they are important, so don't say hurtful things or make rash decisions over a half-day event that will negatively affect real life relationships for years to come.) I used to work for a man who would say, "I could wrestle a bear for a minute," meaning that if he could keep the end of a difficult situation in sight, he could do just about anything.

Second, remember that you can only control your own thoughts and actions; you cannot control other people. Instead of saying to an adult child, "I hate your father and don't you let him bring that #@%&*! to the wedding, or I won't come!" use the approach, "Of course, I would prefer not to have to see your father's new wife, and if he brings her to the wedding, I may feel uncomfortable. But you and your fiancé are important to me. Can we discuss some creative seating arrangement that wouldn't require that I sit next to her or have to interact with her very much?" As my friend Beverly says, "Choose the hill you're willing to die on." If today's not a good day to die, or you can climb to the top of the hill instead of impaling yourself on it, accept the decisions that your adult child and child-in-law make. Then, in much the same way you talk yourself into getting out of bed for work or over to the gym when you really don't feel like it, muster up the courage, poise, and grace to handle a difficult situation for a few hours.

Remember Bill Flatt's advice from the previous chapter? "You can't [let yourself] feel bad about doing the right thing." Again, that doesn't mean it will be easy or that you will be happy or feel great about it. But if it's the right thing to do, then do it. Generally, making it through the wedding day – with low expectations about how perfect it will be – is going to keep you off ulcer medication and make for better relationships with your adult child and your child-in-law for years to come.

The wedding as a transition for parents

Evelyn Duvall, in her ground-breaking research on in-laws during the early 1950s, identifies weddings as "family affairs," and says that involvement in the wedding on any level can actually help parents adjust to their own and their adult child's new role in life. She relates how one mother said that being involved with all the wedding plans set her free from all responsibilities that she'd previously had as a mother.[x] If, as a mother and future mother-in-law, you can use the wedding planning to practice relating to your adult child and future child-in-law adult to adult, it can pave the way for setting and maintaining appropriate boundaries in your relationship.

I like to think of the wedding as a ceremony of emancipation both for adult children and for parents. For children, the wedding ceremony establishes them officially as a new family unit. For the parents, it marks a time of role changes, especially if it's the last child to leave the nest. We have a photograph of my husband and me, watching our son and his new bride drive off after the wedding reception. We are both smiling widely and Ed has his arm around my neck holding a bunch of roses. It doesn't show the tears of joy, relief, and nostalgia I remember we both had, and it doesn't capture the moment right after when Ed turned to me and said, "We're going to Disneyland!"

---

[i] http://www.costofwedding.com/WeddingCost accessed on 20 June 2006.

[ii] Gloria Call Horsley, *In-Laws: A Guide to Extended Family Therapy* (New York: John Wiley & Sons, 1996), 154-5.

[iii] http://www.thefirstdance.com/pdf/StartIdeas.pdf, 6, accessed on 20 June 2006.

[iv] Ibid, 3.

[v] Ibid, 7.

[vi] Camille Russo with Michael Shain, *How to Be the Perfect Mother-in-Law* (Kansas City, MO: Andrews McMeel Publishing,1997), 18.

[vii] Doherty and Thomas, 4.

[viii] Gloria Call Horsley, *The In-Law Survival Guide* (New York: John Wiley & Sons, 1997), 43-59.

[ix] Ibid, 57.

[x] Evelyn Millis Duvall, *In-Laws: Pro and Con* (New York: Association Press, 1954), 317-8.

- 4 -

Boundaries: Leaving and Cleaving and Other Boundary Issues

One element of mother-in-law behavior that came through loud and clear (read that LOUD and CLEAR) is the importance of respecting the marriage boundaries of the grown child and child-in-law.[i] Of the mothers-in-law surveyed, over 87% said they respect the marriage boundaries of their adult children. However, only 55% of the daughters-in-law reported mothers-in-law respecting the boundaries of their marriage (mothers-in-law who also answered as daughters-in-law reported 66%). While the survey sample did not pair specific mothers-in-law with daughters-in-law, it doesn't take a rocket scientist or a statistician to see there's a significant difference of opinion.

What are boundaries?

The Merriam-Webster Dictionary defines "boundary" as "something that indicates or fixes a limit or extent." I (Leanne) like Wikipedia's definition: "A border that encloses a space or an abstract concept." When we use the term "boundary" outside of the relationship context, we may be referring to some sort of physical boundary, such as a fence that divides two pieces of property.

But more often when we talk about boundaries, we are referring to an abstract concept. For instance, the boundary line between Tennessee and North Carolina is well defined in legal terms (abstract concepts) that a surveyor could verify. However, for the most part, there are no physical boundary lines like white chalk marks or fences that indicate where the line is.

Lest you think this relationship boundary stuff is vastly different from other boundary situations, I want to point out that we deal with abstract boundaries in many other circumstances. Probably the biggest difference in relationship boundaries is not that they are abstract, but, unlike state borders that remain relatively stable over time, humans possess a vast ability to change over the span of a lifetime, and so do their boundary lines.

Boundary negotiations
Red light/green light

What makes life so crazy when an adult child marries is that everyone involved is dealing with not just one, but two boundary negotiations:

1) stretching the boundary of the family to include a new person, and
2) drawing and respecting the boundary line around the newly-formed couple as a distinct, separate, and unique family unit.

Let that sink in for a minute. It can amount to a push/pull effect or a "go, go, go!" and then a "stop, stop, stop!" Remember the game "Red Light/Green Light"? When the "traffic cop" said "Green light!" everyone walked as fast as they could to get to the front line. But when the traffic cop said, "Red light!" you were supposed to stop immediately. I hated that game. I was a chubby child and it took me at least a few seconds to overcome inertia and get moving, but once I got moving it was harder than anything to stop! On the one hand, the mother-in-law is expected to draw this new family member to her breast in a warm motherly embrace ("Green light!"), but at the same time let go of the new child-in-law as well as her own adult child ("Red light!")!

That can be very confusing, especially for a first-time mother-in-law. It's confusing for the young couple too, because they are negotiating their own personal boundaries as they adjust to their new, "married" roles as well as working to establish their own family unit boundaries. Not only does the mother-in-law not know the "rules of engagement", so to speak, but the young couple is still trying to figure them out too.

Leaving and cleaving

For those of us schooled in the King James Version of the bible, we recognize this verse from Genesis 2:24: "Therefore a man will leave his father and mother and cleave to his wife and the two shall become one flesh." It's interesting how we see that verse as we move through the span of our lives. For children, the verse is somewhat confusing and sometimes scary. I remember my seven-year old, Sam, telling me after he heard that verse that he didn't want to leave home. Ever. (I knew it wouldn't last and it didn't.) For teens and young adults it means FREEDOM!! Freedom from the chores and rules and oversight and correcting and, well, you get the idea. For newly married couples, it first means "Hurray! We're finally on our own!" and then when the blush of the honeymoon is over and the bills start coming in, it's, "Uh-oh, we're on our own."

Here's the point: Leaving and cleaving takes work. A very small fraction of it takes place after the wedding and on the honeymoon. The real work takes place when the honeymoon is over, literally and figuratively. It takes work on the part of the grown child and his or her new spouse to learn how to play well with each other in the sandbox of life and to accept all the responsibilities and privileges of being adults. No wonder the Israelites were given the commandment: "If a man has recently married, he must not be sent to war or have any other duty laid on him. For one year he is to be free to stay at home and bring happiness to the wife he has married." It took a year of dedicated effort to get to know one another!

Helping a grown child "leave and cleave" takes work on the part of his or her parents, too (especially the mother/mother-in-law). For 18 or 25 years (often plus another 9 months in utero), the mother has nurtured and loved this child, helping him to solve his problems, interpreting the world for him, and helping him to make important life decisions.

From www.CartoonStock.com, used with permission.

Now, the replacement has arrived on the scene, and it's time for the mother to accomplish her next life tasks: 1) to accept her role as second (and –

when children arrive – third, fourth, fifth, etc.) in her child's priorities and, as if that's not enough to make your head spin, 2) to help her grown son or daughter to turn to his or her spouse for those needs. In other words, part of the mother-in-law job description at this phase of life is to teach the child to let go of you and to depend on his or her mate. This mother-in-law task goes more smoothly if you started preparing your child to leave from the moment he or she was born. If you've waited until now to begin, it will take longer and the task will be more difficult though still quite possible.

For your grown children, this time is one of great change, fluctuating emotions, and personal challenges as they begin negotiating the twists and turns of living together, managing a household budget, facing unrealistic expectations of one another, and countless other issues. There is a great temptation for them to feel the pull to home instead of to their mate. Your child may have grown used to coming to you with issues and decisions she now needs to make with her spouse. You may feel good about being "needed" to make daily decisions, but that is not a mother's role now. Your role is to teach, encourage, and mentor your children in their task of leaving and cleaving.

One husband we heard from said he would always respect his mother-in-law for telling his wife, after their first newlywed fight, that she needed to discuss the matter with her husband instead of her mother. One wife said:

"[My mother-in-law] has butted out unless invited in when it comes to marital issues. Even when she was included, she refused to get involved because she insisted it is our business and that we need to work it out our own way. She made us work on our marriage!"

In the next chapter, we talk more about communication but, suffice it to say here, the best rule of thumb is to NEVER offer advice unless asked and then only if pressed for an answer. That may sound a bit harsh to some of you, but bear with us and all will be revealed in the next chapter.

Acceptance and respect

Given that red light/green light effect, it's not so surprising that when we asked the survey participants what makes for a good mother-in-law/child-in-law relationship and what could be done to improve a mother-in-law/child-in-law relationship, the most frequently used words in their comments were "respect" and "acceptance". Those two words clearly reflect the nature of this two-pronged boundary settlement we talked about earlier. The mother-in-law and the child-in-law want to feel accepted as part of the extended family and yet, the young couple in particular, needs to feel respected as their own family. It's not an "either/or" but a "both/and" proposition.

Here are some of their answers to "What makes for a good mother-in-law/child-in-law relationship?" and "What could be done to improve a mother-in-law/child-in-law relationship?

"Accept each others foibles without judging and critical remarks."

"Accept the differences, love and respect."

"Acceptance of each other and genuine caring."

"Acceptance; we all have our limitations and differences."

"Acceptance and tolerance of differences."

"Acceptance and respect of each other... to expect nothing in return."

"Respect and the ability to calmly acknowledge differences."

"Respect the fact your child chose their partner."

"Respect your child's wishes."

"Respect that the mother-in-law is and always will be the mother, BUT the child-in-law is the new spouse and will break the apron strings – your child will love you no less.☺"

"Respect boundaries and never force the child/spouse to choose between mother and spouse."

Sometimes they said "mutual respect," or other words to show that respect must be a two-way street.

"Mutual respect and understanding that you both have a vested interest in the person who caused you to be related to each other."

"Mutual respect for all the roles each other plays."

"Mutual respect for each other's differences and ideas."

"Mutual respect of each other's lives, home, time, and other family members."

"Mutual respect - a recognition of temperaments and godly contributions that are different from each other yet valuable. With my child-in-law, I bite my tongue and mind my business and remember that some things have to simmer awhile to 'take'."

"Respecting one another's decisions and space."

"Respect that goes both ways: the child-in-law respects the mother-in-law's history with her child and the mother-in-law respects the child-in-law's relationship with her/him."

"Respect for her as my husband's mother and respect for us as a couple"

"Respect for each other's differences."

"Respect for one another in the life of the person they share."

"Respecting each other's feelings and keeping your mouth shut when you know you'll say something you will regret."

"Respecting each other's time and personal boundaries."

Common boundary disputes
Grandchildren

While grandchildren offer great blessings in our lives, sometimes a mother-in-law can consciously or inadvertently overstep the authority of her grandchildren's parents and create discord between herself and her son- or daughter-in-law. We'll discuss more in the "Grandmothering Mother-in-Law" chapter, but here's an example of what some daughters-in-law said:

"It would help if she respected the boundaries my husband and I have in place for our marriage and the way we choose to raise our children."

"I wish she would stop being the parent to her grandchildren (our children) while we are present. I wish she would realize that I am the parent now, and these are my children, not just her grandchildren entrusted to my care."

Decisions

I admit it can be challenging to realize that you are no longer in charge of making decisions for your grown children, especially when you think they are wrong. I have permanent bite marks on my tongue and should probably have more than I do. (Not necessarily because I think they have been so wrong, but rather because I have an innate tendency to butt in!)

Are there ever times when a mother-in-law must intervene? Yes. When children and other innocents are in danger. But most issues in which mothers-in-law become embroiled and children-in-law take issue fall far short of that standard. When it comes to decisions about life, your adult children are in charge. Here's a story from an admiring daughter.

"The one thing I think could help improve the mother-in-law/children-in-law relationship is keeping your mouth shut unless you're asked. I eloped and married at 16, had my first child at 18 and my 2nd at 19. My mother never interfered or tried to tell us how to run our lives. She never gave unsolicited advice or criticized us. We have always been close and as I've looked back as I've gotten older, I've wondered many times HOW she managed to keep her thoughts to herself. I'm sure she had to

bite her tongue many times. :-) I try to do the same with my kids and hope that I can be half the mother and mother-in-law that my Mom is."

Holidays

One child-in-law said one thing s/he would like for the mother-in-law to stop is:

"Not letting us make our own decisions about visiting with extended family over our very few vacation days every year."

A few words about holidays. Sometimes the holiday movies, advertising, recipe books, and every other media make holiday expectations into something quite unrealistic. You have probably had one or two of those "less than perfect" times yourself. But if Jimmy or Susie announces they are going to the other parents' home for a holiday, wish them a wonderful visit. It doesn't mean you have to like it and it doesn't mean you can't cry.

Here's where that supportive spouse or friend comes in: cry on their shoulders. Tell them how sad it will be not to have your traditional family eggnog on Christmas Eve and how you will miss them at the extended family Christmas brunch. Tell them how hard this transition is for you and how much you don't like it. But let your child and child-in-law enjoy a guilt-free holiday. Or here's another idea: celebrate the holiday on another day. If the children and children-in-law won't be there for Thanksgiving Day, have your celebration on the Saturday before.[ii] Who knows, maybe you'll start a new family tradition?

Where to spend the holidays is a boundary negotiation, and releasing your child-in-law from that requirement may actually improve your mother-in-law/child-in-law relationship. The survey shows that approximately 27% of the mothers-in-law surveyed expect their adult children and family to spend at least part of every holiday with them; 26% of the children-in-law agree with that expectation. However, in general, those children-in-law whose mothers-in-law do not expect them to spend every holiday with them were more likely to report that they had a good relationship with their mother-in-law.

Home

The physical boundaries of home must remain sacrosanct. Sure, I know of mothers who have keys to their adult children's homes, and if that works for BOTH child and child-in-law, that's fine. But if either of the couple doesn't like that arrangement, stop it. Immediately. It's important for young couples to establish their own identity as a family, and one very important realm in which that is played out is in the home. By establishing that identity, men and women learn to establish authority over themselves as a couple and later as a family when children are added.

Even if the couple and mother/mother-in-law agree about her possessing a key, they would be wise to design some limits, such as calling ahead of time – if not for the adult children, then to protect the mother/mother-in-law from embarrassment herself. One young couple said:

> *"We wish she would stop walking into our house unexpectedly. Not that we mind her coming because it is not that often; we just walk around in our underwear a lot."*

Money

If, as the good book tells us, the love of money is the root of all evil, then surely the control of money is the root of all conflict. Nowhere can that be seen more dramatically than in issues surrounding the giving and receiving of money and money advice in in-law relationships. Two comments serve to underscore that point:

"I wish she would stop trying to push things onto us that she thinks we need and we don't want – particularly when we can't afford it so she attempts to pay – then it would be easier for us to be seen as adults. It will be nice when we can be completely financially stable on our own and then I don't have to find polite ways to decline all the support on things we don't want."

"She tries to get us to live our lives the way she does as an established, 50+ year old woman, even if we cannot afford to do so at this stage in our lives. With such a low income we really can't afford great health insurance or a retirement/investment fund but she doesn't seem to understand this and is always pushing us to take care of these issues. I wish she didn't always feel like we need what she has, even if it means being financially dependent on her."

As you can see from the above comments, the giving of money, whether the mother/mother-in-law intends so or not, can be seen as an indictment that the young couple are not seen as adults and may communicate a lack of confidence in their abilities to take care of themselves. That can sting particularly badly if your son or son-in-law gets that message.

Does that mean you can't ever give them money? Certainly not, but it must be tempered with the other messages (control, power, lack of faith in them, etc.) inextricably linked to the money you are giving them. If they tell you to stop, then stop. If you still want to assist, discuss the matter with your adult child and child-in-law, but in the end, abide by their wishes.

In addition, once that money passes from your hands to theirs, it no longer belongs to you. You may give it for a certain reason, you may request that it be used in a certain manner, but once you give it, it becomes their property. You cannot control that money any longer. You can choose not to give them money in the future, but you have no control over any monies that have already changed hands. Sometimes parents of adult children have a hard time dealing with that reality. If you are one of them, re-read this section.

Son/husband

As mentioned above, expressing distrust of a son's or son-in-law's adulthood or abilities should be avoided at every turn. People rarely excel when criticized, but often reach for new heights of excellence when praised. A mother who undermines her own son's or son-in-law's integrity by belittling

his efforts not only does harm to her relationship with
him, but also corrodes his authority with his children
and relationship with his wife. We've devoted a
whole chapter to sons-in-law, but some of the
comments we received are worth including here:

> *"My mother-in-law would harp on my husband when
> he was out of work and make him feel worse than he
> was already feeling and I ultimately got the raw end
> of that. . . ."*

> *"I wish she would let my 46 year old husband be a
> man. She tells him what to do all the time about
> everything. Everything!!! They and his sister work
> together; they both control him. He doesn't see it."*

> *"I wish she was able to `allow` her son to cleave to
> his adult family, rather than thinking we need to be
> enthralled with her life."*

> *"[I would like for my mother-in-law] to value and
> respect her son for who he is instead of having some
> image of him falling short."*

Time

Issues of time become another boundary
negotiation, often regardless of how close or far the

distance. Most of the children-in-law in the survey (in fact, almost 70%) didn't think their in-laws called or visited too often. Here are some sample answers to the question "What would you like your mother-in-law to do more?"

"Call/Visit more often."

"Come and stay with us when she visits."

"Come out to visit us more."

"Come to my house, instead of us always coming to hers. We just live 7 minutes away and she could be more involved with our day-to-day stuff if she saw us `in action`...besides, packing up my little ones is harder right now."

"I wish she were able to spend more time with us."

"Visit or call more often, even for a few minutes or whatever."

"Visit us and the children at our house more often."

In fact, almost 20% of the children-in-law answering that question expressed a desire for MORE interaction (time) with the mother-in-law. But the 30% of those who believed their mothers-in-law visited too often didn't necessarily dislike being with their mothers-in-law, but they did want less time with her. Here's one example:

> *"I would LOVE it if she called a lot less. We live only 25 minutes away and we see her and my father-in-law often. Lots of times, I feel like I don't have enough `family` time with just my spouse and our daughter because the in-laws are always checking in and want to know what's going on all the time...kinda like busy bodies...they don't have enough going on in their own lives."*

Respecting the time a couple has together can be a tangible way to honor their marriage and family commitments. Today, in many families, both husband and wife work, leaving precious little time for family interaction and, when there are children, even less for couple time. Often, time to themselves to recharge their own batteries is sorely missing.

My daughter has chosen to be a stay-at-home mom and, in addition, she home schools their children. Because she's at home during the day, many people assume she has a lot of time on her hands, but she basically works non-stop from the time the baby wakes up in the morning until she falls into bed at night. When I call her, I've learned to ask, "Is this a good time to talk for a few minutes?" If not, we arrange a time for me to get back with her and I talk to her then.

Setting time boundaries, however, is the responsibility of both the mother-in-law and the adult child and child-in-law. Mothers-in-law must be respectful, that is true. But, the child and child-in-law need to make her aware of interferences. Sometimes I hear young women complain about how their mother or mother-in-law does annoying things and yet, when I ask if she has made her mother or mother-in-law aware of those things, I get a blank stare and/or she tells me "Well, no, but she knows what she's doing."

One of the issues I dealt with in the Navy was the problem of confronting. Somehow we've developed an aversion to lovingly confronting another person and speaking our hearts. Oh, yes, we can "speak our minds" in an angry way, but many people have trouble confronting conflict and dealing with it in an open and loving fashion. That's probably why we see so many websites spewing out venom towards mothers-in-law: they haven't figured out the "art" of loving confrontation. People cannot read our minds!

We must use words to give them that insight. In so doing, we are setting boundaries for others to follow. I've heard it said, "Time and distance don't diminish relationships; hurt and anger do." Just make sure your time and distance boundaries are not the reason for the hurt and anger.

Unsolicited advice and criticism

Another element of boundary negotiation that warrants mentioning is that hardest of all things to control: our tongues. It's really no wonder there were so many comments from participants about "respecting differences" because "where there are differences, there are potential problems, which often surface as criticisms."[iii]

When we asked the survey participants, only between 17% and 35% (depending on the number of children-in-law they have) of the mothers-in-law owned up to giving unsolicited advice or criticism, while 54% of the children-in-law reported they were on the receiving end of advice and criticism. That finding is also substantiated in other studies where mothers-in-law report that behavior less often than children-in-law.[iv] Of course, the sample did not match specific mothers-in-law and children-in-law, but it shows that perhaps either mothers-in-law are giving more than they realize, children-in-law are hearing what is said as advice or criticism when that wasn't the intent, or both.

Another researcher calls it the "Rashomon Principle" in honor of a Japanese movie where four people saw the same crime and all described it in different ways.[v] I call it the "beach ball effect;" we may all be looking at a beach ball, but because we see it from different sides, we all see different colors. We hear and see situations, people, and things with the sum total of our experiences. What might sound like an innocent statement to you such as, "Wow, that rose bush is tall!" might spark a defensive response in me such as, "Well I really haven't had time to do any yard work this week." Those misunderstandings occur more frequently if there is a history of unresolved conflict or tension in the relationship. They can also occur early in the relationship when neither the mother-in-law nor the child-in-law knows one another very well.

These children-in-law completed the sentence "I wish my mother-in-law would stop…":

"Telling me how to do things."

"Constantly suggesting things as though I do not have a brain and cannot think for myself."

"Trying to be a mentor who dishes out sage advice."

"Maybe being so harsh with her advice. Sometimes it is hard to take. She is very outspoken and does not hide her feelings. I am the opposite and part of me admires that but the other part would not ever say some of the things she says. If she says something she feels is inappropriate, she will later call and apologize though. It's just how she is."

One mother-in-law offered this:

"I think mothers-in-law should keep communication open, not criticizing, and offering advice (mother-in-law) mainly just when asked for it. That's been hard for me with my grown children as well as their spouses sometimes."

Border patrol

So, how do we patrol the border either during or after we negotiate a boundary agreement? We humans use words, geographical distance, time, emotional distance, and even other people to define our boundaries. Open communication and effective conflict resolution (at the earliest possible signs of a boundary problem) can keep from building walls of resentment caused by unresolved hurt and anger.

Probably the single most important factor in maintaining good relationships is being intentional about what we do. So often we go on "autopilot" when it comes to relationships. Instead of paying attention, we assume. I learned early in my Navy career: to assume "makes an 'a**' out of 'u' and 'me'." Never go on autopilot. Oh, sure, it works for a time. But, just like an airplane, if you don't pay attention, the plane runs out of fuel and crashes. The same is true of relationships. We must patrol our own boundaries and make sure we continue to respect the boundaries of others, especially our children-in-law, if we want to continue good relations.

---

[i] This correlates with research done in 1954, which also indicated that mothers-in-law as "the most difficult in-law" mettled, interfered, and intruded on privacy, all of which are boundary issues.

[ii] Annie Chapman, *The Mother-in-Law Dance* (Eugene, OR: Harvest House, 2004), 65.

[iii] Laurie E. Rozakis, *The Complete Idiot's Guide to Dealing with In-Laws* (New York: Alpha Books, 1998), 30.

[iv] Helene S. Arnstein, *Between Mothers-in-Law and Daughters-in-Law* (New York: Dodd, Mead & Co., 1985), 75.

[v] Ibid, 81-82.

- 5 -

Communication: Making Sweet the Words I May Have to Eat

We can't *not* communicate. Just like we can't *not* breathe. If you think about it, even saying nothing is saying something. Therapists often have couples come into their offices and say, "We just don't communicate," but that is not so. They may not be communicating very well, they may be arguing, or they might not even be speaking to one another, but they are communicating. Just try not speaking to your spouse or your best friend for a week and I guarantee they will have an idea you have communicated something to them!

Cartoon copyrighted by Mark Parisi, printed with permission.

When we asked children-in-law about their mothers-in-law, communication figured prominently in their answers. Here's what they had to say.

Listening

"I wish my mother-in-law would listen actively and attentively."

"I wish she would listen more genuinely."

"I wish she would listen to us when we talk about what we like."

"I wish she would actively listen and understand my feelings."

"It would be good if she tried to listen in ANY conversation and it not end up being about her...."

"I wish she was a better listener and comfortable with talking about serious issues; it would make me feel more comfortable to talk with her about anything."

These statements reflect the sentiments of hundreds of children-in-law who responded to the survey, and they underscore the importance of listening in effective communication. You see, people often get confused about what communication means. When we say someone is a "great communicator," we're usually referring to someone's ability to verbally express herself well. But the process of communication is only complete when there's an active listener on the other end. If I don't listen to what you are saying, we have failed to communicate.

In fact, effective communication only takes place when the speaker speaks, and the listener listens and gives feedback to the speaker to indicate what message was received. Sort of like this:

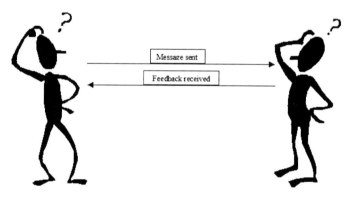

But of the ways we choose to communicate, our words do not carry the greatest impact. That honor goes to the non-verbal realm.

Communication researchers tell us, in fact, that about 55% of the "message" we send in any communication travels through our non-verbal expressions (facial expressions, body language, etc.) Tone of voice (including volume and inflection) accounts for about 38% of the communicated message, leaving words as the least important and thereby the least reliable means of communicating. But that doesn't mean words aren't important; it just means that words are not sufficient to carry the day.

What if I have an argument with my husband and – when I go to apologize to him – I clench my fists, grit my teeth, and say in a strained tone of voice, "I'm sorry!"? I may have the words right, but my tone of voice and probably my body language shout a very different message. In order for a message to be clear, all three forms of communication must be in sync. If any one of them is different, an individual may hear a very different message than the sender intended.

Filters

How does this relate to mother-in-law/child-in-law relationships? We know that sometimes, even with the best intentions, the message sent and the message received are two different things, because we filter everything we hear and see through the sum total of our experiences. Something like this:

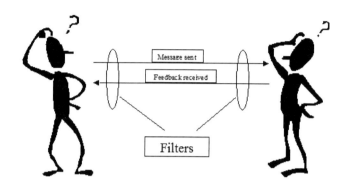

One child-in-law said:

"[I wish my mother-in-law would] try to get to know me and appreciate me for who I really am. Sometimes she does this and is pleasantly surprised by what she learns, but she has made too many weird and inaccurate assumptions over the years that I don't think she has any idea of the person I really am."

Maybe this mother-in-law had some of her own "filters" in place when she made those "weird and inaccurate assumptions" about her child-in-law.

Take for example the case of tattoos. When I (Leanne) was growing up, my father was in the Navy and the only tattoos I saw were on the sailors who worked for him or those I happened to see around the base. My family tradition said respectable people don't get tattoos. But guess what? The world has changed, and all sorts of young people get tattoos now, many of them good, honest, hard-working professionals, and faithful and honest Christians. If I allow my (now outdated) message about tattoos to filter how I see and respond to someone, I might be working off some wrong and damaging assumptions.

The key here is, the more aware I am of my own filters, the better able I am to turn them on and off. Of course, we need filters for some things. If I am walking down a dark alley in a high crime neighborhood at night and I see a man approaching me with a gun, my filters will tell me to fight or flee (I think I would choose to flee!), so filters are not all bad. We just need to be aware of them and, unless we are in a high threat situation, question them or turn them off.

Also, the better we know another person and the better we understand her filters, the better able we are to effectively communicate with her. Take, for example, a daughter-in-law who grew up in an abusive household. She may view a loud and animated discussion of politics as a potentially dangerous situation, and may respond to it as if it were. Unless I know her well enough to understand her reaction, I might draw assumptions about her that are false, such as "She must disagree with my political opinions," or "She isn't interested in politics."

Five levels of communication

So, the better we know a person, the more likely we will be able to understand her filters and also communicate with her on a deeper level. We communicate on five levels[i]:

> **Level 1 - Clichés and polite exchanges.** Examples include, "Way to go!" "Good Job!" and "How are you today?" "Fine, and you?"
> **Level 2 – Sharing information.** Examples include "I washed the car today," "We're having veal for supper," and "I think Polly has chicken pox." (Unfortunately, this is where most married couples get stuck, especially during the child-rearing years.)
> **Level 3 – Involves sharing opinions, judgments, and ideas.** Examples include, "I approve of what Senator Moore is doing about transportation costs," and "Billy is wrong to

expect Joe to lie for him," and "I have a dream of being a portrait artist someday."

Level 4 – Involves sharing feelings and emotions. Examples would be, "When you yell at me, I feel hurt and afraid," and "I feel sad about Janie moving so far away from home."

Level 5 – Referred to as "Peak communication" or "true intimacy" and is reserved for married couples, close family members, or the closest friends. When we use peak communication, we are able to travel up and down through the different levels of communication without fear of being attacked, misunderstood, etc.

As you can see, each step into the level of communication is a bit more risky than the one before in terms of exposing our true nature to someone else. Each step makes us more vulnerable to another person and hence a sense of safety or trust must be developed before that level can be fully shared.

Can you discuss difficult problems?

When we asked survey respondents if they could discuss difficult problems with their mothers-in-law, 30% of the daughters-in-law and 44% of the sons-in-law indicated they could. Being able to discuss difficult issues would seem to indicate these children-in-law are able to communicate on a deeper level with their mothers-in-law. We did not ask about the "quality" of those discussions (such as, were they arguments or quiet problem-solving sessions), but it appears that those children-in-law who can talk with their mothers-in-law on that level do report better mother-in-law/child-in-law relationships.

Some respondents reflect a movement to deeper levels of "knowing" with their mothers-in-law in these statements:

"I've known her since I was a young teenager (when my husband and I started dating). She always was willing to talk about difficult subjects and treat me as her own. She was/is like a mother to me."

"She can make me look at my shortcomings in a positive way that allows me to grow. She says we all have to deal with issues and disappointments in our lives; it's the way we choose to handle them that molds our character and who we become."

"My mom has different priorities sometimes, and often tells me she wants to be my friend more than my mom. My mother-in-law understands what my

husband and I want from life and supports us, so sometimes when I have problems with my mom, I can go to my mother-in-law and feel like I have a mom and that is a huge comfort."

Listening (again)

How can you move from surface or "acquaintance" communication to a deeper level of sharing? Here's what some of the respondents said about their mothers-in-law:

"She listens if I need to talk."

"She listens and is always there for us."

"We are able to have great conversations."

"She can be very good to talk to, like a girlfriend."

Researchers tell us we only hear about 50-75% of what is said to us because the rest of the time we are thinking about our response. This is especially true if we have preconceived ideas about the speaker or have strong filters in place. Actively listening to another person requires focus and a conscious effort to put our own thoughts aside.

A helpful exercise used by many marriage therapists to foster active listening is to have couples do what's called "active and reflective listening," where one person speaks and his or her partner "reflects back" or paraphrases what has been said. If the couple is not told ahead of time that they will have to paraphrase the thought of the other partner, many times they are unable to accurately restate their partner's thought. Even when they are told in advance, couples often remark how difficult it is to stay focused on what their partner is saying and not on formulating a response.

So listening, truly listening, is a skill to be mastered. Try this experiment. The next time your son-in-law (spouse, friend, child, daughter-in-law, etc.) tells you something, listen very carefully and then paraphrase back what he said. If your son-in-law tells you about his day, rather than telling him about yours, "reflect back" as in, "Oh boy, it sounds like you really had a busy day today with all those sales reps visiting," and keep the conversation going about him for a while, each time listening carefully and validating what he is saying. When you do this, you are keeping the focus on him and, by the way, getting to know him better.

When we asked children-in-law what they would like their mothers-in-law to do more, here's what they said:

"A little more open-ness about her personal feelings, aside from her feelings about her son... like life things."

"If she was a better listener and comfortable with talking about serious issues, it would make me feel more comfortable to talk to her about anything."

"Actively listen to understand my feelings."

"Actually follow up comments of 'How are you?' with concern."

"Have a real conversation that concerns something other than herself."

"Focus on the value of family and communication as a family; closeness and togetherness."

"Be able to talk and have an honest and open relationship."

"Have a friendly conversation."

"Be able to talk and understand each other without any hidden motives/agenda."

"Be comfortable enough with each other to tease, laugh, joke, and be together (without the spouse present)."

"Call and talk to me instead of just talking to my husband."

"Call just to say hi and not expect it to turn into an invitation to spend time together."

"Call just to visit with me."

"Call or email me more often."

"Engage in long, funny conversations."

"Sit and visit, without planning activities to do."

"Talk about herself and her personal feelings."

"Talk to me and let me know what she's really feeling."

"*Talk to me like a friend.*"

"*Talk to me honestly.*"

"*Tell funny stories and laugh out loud.*"

"*Tell jokes, and be more laid back.*"

"*I wish that she had more motherly talks with me and said hello to me when she talks to my husband on the phone.*"

"*Invite me to spend time just with her. I feel like sometimes I have to initiate this contact.*"

"*I wish she would call just to say hi without having some big crisis that she needs to talk to my husband about.*"

"*Initiate a closer relationship with me.*"

"*Just hang out with us. We love having her around.*"

"*Just sit and talk without the suggestions.*"

"Laugh. Show some vulnerability. Talk softly and gently now and again. Reveal her humanity -- the fear of growing old. Relax and enjoy life and us and her grandkids."

"Listen attentively and actively."

"Listen more genuinely."

"Listen to us when we talk about what we like."

"Try to be a friend who enjoys time together as equals and discusses matters from a position of mutual respect."

To give you an opportunity to listen to your daughter-in-law and share with her, we've included a conversation guide just before the appendices. There are things to consider before you talk to your daughter-in-law and questions to guide you in sharing your thoughts and opinions.

Communication problems

Of course, some children-in-law reported communication problems with their mothers-in-law:

"She calls mostly when she is depressed."

"She calls all the time."

"She calls at times when we are busy, and stays on the phone for a long time (e.g., being disrespectful of my wife's and my time)."

"Her current lifestyle requires dramatic change to have any positive impact on our relationship. Unfortunately, our mother-in-law/daughter-in-law relationship is nonexistent until then (except for fake pleasantries for the sake of `peace` at family gatherings)."

"I wish we could have a conversation. Instead, she'd ask a question, then cut in mid-reply to ask another, etc., never hearing what she was asking for--real crazy-making."

"I would like for her to stop asking us highly personal questions (including baby plans); also for her to stop answering for my husband when I ask him a question."

"She talks about us behind our back to our friends. If she has a problem, she should come directly to us."

"She uses passive aggressive manipulation...'No, that's ok. I don't mind if you can't come to Sunday dinner. I'm just an old woman and I know you'll have more fun without me.'"

"Her gossiping about everyone's business. She is not good to let know your business."

"I have been and will continue to say sweet, loving things to my mother-in-law consistently. If she would occasionally say something nice back I'd be ecstatic."

"If she tried to listen in ANY conversation and it not end up being about her, and that her problem or circumstance is always bigger, better or badder than anyone else's. She thrives on topping everyone else's life with her own."

"If she called more often during the day to check in on me and our son, so we could have everyday conversations. Right now we only talk to them about once every 6 or so weeks and the phone conversation is LONG and meaningless...it's just a bunch of catch up on THEIR lives."

"If she could open up more and share her feelings in a vulnerable way instead of always bossing everyone around and making demands: if she could learn to receive love."

Generally, we enjoy being with people with whom we can be ourselves, laugh, talk, and feel safe. Our survey indicated 48% of the daughters-in-law[ii] and 64% of the sons-in-law agreed that they enjoyed spending time with their mothers-in-law. Those children-in-law were also highly likely to say they had good relationships with their mothers-in-law. It makes sense; if you enjoy doing things with your mother-in-law, that is probably an indicator of a good relationship and vice versa.

Praise and criticism
The power of praise
One element of interpersonal communication that can't be stressed enough is the power of praise. It serves as one of the "Five Love Languages,"[iii] and often is the oil that keeps any relationship train running smoothly on its tracks. Praise brightens a child's face like almost nothing else. When researchers looked into what motivates employees the most, it wasn't money, Christmas hams, parking spaces, or window offices that boosted their egos.

What motivates employees the most is a personal hand-written note from their boss saying, "Well done!" In the words of the *One Minute Manager*, "Catch someone doing something right and reward him for it!"[iv] The same is true for our personal relationships, including those with our adult children and children-in-law.

Fifty-five percent of daughter-in-law survey participants indicated they receive unsolicited praise from their mothers-in-law, while 62% of the sons-in-law reported the same.[v] Here's an example from one child-in-law:

> *"She is so supportive and never passes up a chance to tell me that she loves me and is glad I'm a part of the family."*

Here are some comments from participants about encouragement and praise when asked what would improve mother-in-law/child-in-law relationships:

> *"Praise her son for the great things he does and stop focusing on how to fix him."*

"A relationship in which each party appreciates the strengths of the other, and doesn't criticize their weaknesses."

"Express her pride in my husband."

"Tell my husband she is proud of him. He is always helping her with their lawn or in the store that his parents own, and his parents are always critical of him. If his mother were to thank him for it now and again, I would feel so much better about it."

"Encourage my husband and be more supportive of where we live."

"My husband's mother is a Godly woman, and I believe she could benefit her sons and their families to a greater capacity by expressing her support and encouragement with more positive input."

"Offer praise more often, especially to grandchildren."

"I would love for her to tell my husband how proud she is of him. She only says positive things about him to others."

"If my mother-in-law openly valued her son and respected his choices, rather than criticize more, I think he would be happier and would feel more fulfilled. I would appreciate her more."

"If she could understand MY giftedness - could recognize/affirm any good things I have done."

"Praise me (genuinely)."

"Praise me instead of (or in addition to) her child."

"Tell me good things about my husband/her son...instead of the things she feels he does wrong or should change."

"Tell me that she appreciates me."

"Compliment her daughters-in law more often."

"Compliment my cooking and housecleaning."

The curse of criticism

Noted relationship researcher John Gottman once predicted that he could listen to a couple talk for five minutes and predict whether or not they were headed for a divorce. And he was right a majority of the time. From that research, he determined that we humans need a ratio of about five positive communications (praise, appreciation, loving words, etc.) to every one negative communication (criticism, blaming, angry words, etc.) in order for us to keep our emotional "bank account" with that person from going into the danger zone.[vi]

When we asked survey participants, we noticed a disparity between mothers-in-law and children-in-law (particularly daughters-in-law) concerning the giving and receiving of "unsolicited advice and criticism." Fifty-four percent of daughters-in-law (and 44% of sons-in-law) said their mothers-in-law give unsolicited advice and criticism. But only 17-35% of mothers-in-law reported that behavior.[vii] Since the survey did not match particular mothers-in-law and daughters-in-law, it's possible that we just got answers from the mothers-in-law who don't give unsolicited advice and criticism.

However, it's also possible that children-in-law hear advice and criticism in more comments than mothers-in-law realize. In fact, only 45% of the children-in-law said they could listen to their mother-in-law's opinions without feeling criticized while 80% of the mothers-in-law said they could. Or, mothers-in-law may be criticizing more than they realize and building walls instead of windows. Here are some of the comments received:

"I wish she would stop giving her advice or opinions that are not asked for or warranted."

"She criticizes my abilities as a wife."

"She criticizes how I raise my daughter."

"[My mother-in-law] criticizes my beliefs on personal matters."

"She criticizes how we handle our dog."

"She criticizes everything I do."

With that in mind, it would seem prudent for every mother-in-law to concentrate on giving her child-in-law as many positive strokes as possible. That way, if – and it's a big IF – she ever needs to admonish, constructively criticize, or even make "suggestions," her child-in-law's emotional bank account can take the withdrawal.

But what if you run into real conflict? Our survey respondents helped us with that issue too. Just turn to the next chapter.

[i] Gary Smalley, *Secrets To Lasting Love : Uncovering The Keys To Lifelong Intimacy* (New York: Fireside, 2000).

[ii] Mother-in-law who also answered the survey as daughter-in-law indicated 59%.

[iii] Gary Chapman, *The Five Love Languages: How to Express Heartfelt Commitment to Your Mate* (Chicago, IL: Moody Publishers, 1992).

[iv] Kenneth Blanchard and Spencer Johnson, *The One-Minute Manager* (New York: Berkley Books, 1981), 38-39.

[v] Eighty-two percent of the mothers-in-law who answered our survey indicated they gave unsolicited praise to their children-in-law. We may be seeing a "filter" in place that deflects what would be considered a praise, or a sampling issue in that the mothers-in-law who answered our survey were more interested in good mother-in-law relationships and actually do give their own children-in-law praise more often than the children-in-law who participated in our study. The amount of unsolicited praise given to mothers-in-law was more consistent between our populations. Sixty percent of the daughters-in-law and 62% of the sons-in-law said they give their mothers-in-law unsolicited praise, while 60% of the mothers-in-law report receiving praise from their children-in-law.

[vi] John Gottman, *Why Marriages Succeed or Fail* (New York: Simon & Schuster, 1994).

[vii] We list the responses in a range because the mothers-in-law that answered report giving less unsolicited advice and criticism the more children-in-law that she has. Approximately 35% of the mothers-in-law with one child-in-law report advising and criticizing; with two, 25%, and with three, 17%.

- 6 -

Conflict Resolution: Discord and Harmony

World conflict. Marital conflict. Family conflict. Conflict is part of life. And as long as there are at least two people residing on this planet, one of them will think differently from the other. Sometimes we even feel conflict within ourselves regarding what we think or feel about a given situation or topic. And conflict is not all bad. A few days ago, my (Leanne's) son-in-law shared a quote from Eric Hoffer, a 20th century social writer, which says, "The beginning of thought is disagreement – not only with others, but with ourselves." So conflict or disagreement can actually spur us to think more deeply about issues and perhaps come up with a solution we would not have seriously considered without disagreement.

Take, for example, the issue of money. Some people are savers while others are spenders. (Interestingly, these two different money personality types often end up marrying each other.) That represents a conflict. However, if – instead of trying to force one opinion on the other – the couple decides to try and learn from the other, the result might mean a gain for both. The saver may learn how to spend a little more and use money either helping others or purchasing things that make life a bit easier for the family. The spender may learn to save and help provide more financial security for the family. Effective resolution of the conflict can actually spur each to grow and stretch in ways they may not have even considered on their own.

So, if conflict is so good, how can it often end up making people feel so bad? The key, of course, is in how we handle the conflict. But before we get to the how, let's learn a little about some of the causes of conflict in in-law relationships.

Reasons for Conflict

Earlier studies show that conflicts between in-laws occur in some fairly predictable arenas. Lifestyles, customs, and values; generational differences; personality differences; sibling and child-in-law rivalry; differences in working and non-working mother-in-law and daughter-in-law;[i] overstepping the couple's marital boundaries by being "meddlesome," possessive, jealous, or nagging; intruding (not respecting the couple's time or space by calling or visiting too often);[ii] child-rearing differences;[iii] and differences over household chores and management.

Some of these areas stem from differences in background and beliefs, yet others seem to focus on negative or destructive behaviors. While the two could be linked (a belief that leads to a certain behavior), it may be useful to "pull the string" on that idea. By tracing a conflict back to its source, you may gain some insight into its nature that might help you in trying to resolve it. Think back to a time of conflict between you and your child-in-law. Did the conflict stem from a difference in background, beliefs, or opinions? Or was the conflict based on some action or behavior (yours and/or theirs)?

off the mark.com   by Mark Parisi

Cartoon copyrighted by Mark Parisi, printed with permission.

Our survey participants echoed what some of the earlier studies indicated. When we asked children-in-law what their mother-in-law did that they would like for them to stop doing (roughly equivalent to what causes conflict), here's what they said:

I would like for my mother-in-law to stop...
- *Complaining*
- *Undermining the child-in-law's discipline of the children*
- *Not facing problems and discussing them*
- *Criticizing husband/son, child-in-law, or child-in-law's family*
- *Voting for [the other political party]*
- *Perfectionism*
- *Criticizing decisions the couple makes*
- *Trying to "be in control"*
- *Being "self-centered" or "self-absorbed"*
- *Having a negative attitude*
- *Worrying*
- *Giving money or time but with conditions*
- *Not treating the child-in-law with respect*
- *Calling too much*
- *Not calling enough*
- *Not respecting the marriage boundaries in terms of time or intruding on decisions the couple has made*
- *Showing favoritism between children, child-in-law, and/or grandchildren*
- *Making excuses for other family members*
- *Being manipulative*
- *Lying (about her children, child-in-law, and herself)*

- *Destructive personal habits such as smoking and drug use or excessive drinking, and extra-marital affairs*

The list is varied and sometimes contradictory. But again you can see that some of the issues raised may stem from background, beliefs, or opinions while others clearly describe behaviors. Can you identify with anything on the above list? Has your adult child or child-in-law said or indicated they would like for you to stop doing something? Do you and your child-in-law have differences? Do you disagree on anything?

Ways of Resolving Conflict

No matter how you get into a conflict or what the conflict is about, there are a variety of ways to resolve it. Some of the ways listed below actually draw people closer to one another; some drive the wedge between them deeper. These are the ways our survey respondents told us they resolve (or don't resolve) conflict.

Conflict avoidance

Avoiding conflict altogether may, at first glance, look like an appealing way to handle difficult situations. However, many people avoid conflict either because they don't know how to approach conflict or because they do not feel safe enough to voice their opinion. Avoiding conflict for those reasons, especially about important matters, may actually drive the wedge further between two people.

Take a look at what some of our survey participants said about conflict avoidance and see if it looks like these relationships are closer or more conflicted.

What mothers-in-law said about conflicts with their children-in-law:

"Conflicts are not resolved, he won't talk to me if he's mad; he wants to avoid conflict."

"My daughter-in-law usually drops the issue before it's resolved because she doesn't like conflict."

"They aren't resolved. I don't feel comfortable or safe in discussing incidences when I've felt offended or hurt by my daughter-in-law's comments or actions."

"We avoid talking. I keep my distance and keep my mouth shut."

"We visit every 6-8 weeks (live in far cities) – we now ignore conflicts."

"If a problem is brought to light, my daughter-in-law and son just look at me with tolerance. It doesn't seem they want to have forgiveness or love pass between us."

What children-in-law said about their mothers-in-law:

"We avoid conflicts--just don't bring up problems--pretend they didn't happen."

"Conflicts are not discussed after a difference is discovered. [My mother-in-law] will shut down."

"We don't confront each other. I usually act as if nothing is wrong."

"Either everyone has to pretend nothing happened or if I do say something I am ignored and not spoken to."

"Issues are mostly overlooked until it is water under the bridge."

"She has no filter in her brain for realizing when her thoughts should not be spoken. She is pressuring my husband and me to have children, and it is driving a wedge between us. I avoid her at all cost because I never know what embarrassing question she is going to ask me next... conflicts are not being resolved, because she never knows she has said anything offensive. We live in different states, so I put up with it when in her presence. When I am with my husband, I unload a little! When I am with my girlfriends, I unload a lot! Conflicts aren't resolved; I just avoid her."

"Bottling it up"

"Stuffing it" or "bottling it up" has much in common with both avoiding conflict and with anger (discussed shortly). The conflict is alive and waiting just below the surface, until the proverbial last straw lands on the camel's back and the façade of peace collapses. Bottled up anger, or anger turned inward, hurts us spiritually, emotionally, and physically, and it can manifest itself in depression, anxiety, headaches, high blood pressure, nausea, intestinal disorders, and alcohol and drug use.[iv] It works on us like those larvae that have killed many of the live oaks in the U.S., from the inside out. Yet, several of our survey respondents say this is how they handle conflict with their in-laws. How would you describe their relationships?

From mothers-in-law:

"I tolerate my daughter-in-law for the sake of my relationship with my son and grandchildren."

"My son and daughter-in-law are not actually married, but they are raising our grandson together and are engaged. Before the baby came, my daughter-in-law and I got along great. Afterwards, she became angry at me, did not want to be around me, and cursed me out for things I had not done. I still love her very much and all is forgiven. Things seem to be a bit better, but my son does not feel that he can show much affection for me, because it seems to make my daughter-in-law angry. All I want is for us all to love each other. I just try very hard not to say or do anything that can be misunderstood and cause conflict. In other words, I pretty much walk on eggshells."

And from the children-in-law:

"I avoid conflicts –I shut up and leave if one arises - then fume!"

"I keep it bottled up inside. My mother-in-law will directly confront us if she doesn't like our behavior or something we do. If we disagree, then we are wrong, and that's why I don't say anything most of the time."

"I just listen and listen and listen and bite my tongue. Then we leave and I go on."

"I SUCK IT UP."

"I usually just end up giving in which leaves me boiling inside."

"Nothing is ever really resolved I guess. Time just covers it up."

Putting spouse in the middle

Some of those who answered our survey seemed to think that allowing the adult child to talk with his/her mother about a difficult issue might be the best approach, especially early in the mother-in-law/child-in-law relationship. Sometimes it's easier to discuss issues with a son or daughter with whom you have a longer history and a stronger relationship than with a child-in-law, especially if the issue is a sensitive one. However, the goal should be, over time, to establish a one-on-one relationship with your child-in-law, so you will both feel freer to talk out issues between you. The participants we heard from express both positive and negative views of this arrangement.

Mothers-in-law said:

"[I discuss things] first with my son and then with my daughter-in-law. We haven't had much conflict!"

"My daughter-in-law speaks to my son and he speaks to me. Then I talk with her about it to resolve it quickly. We both have thought the best of each other from day one, so it's usually a misunderstanding, not a major problem."

And from children-in-law:

"I do not confront her...if there is a conflict between us, I may talk to my husband about it and then I just try to get over it."

"*My wife mainly works to resolve conflicts with her mother.*"

"*I speak to my husband and if necessary he speaks to her about the conflict.*"

"*My husband is the go between. If she has a problem with me she tells him, not me.*"

"*[We deal with conflict] by me talking to my husband so my husband tells my mother-in-law. He feels he can communicate with her better since he has been dealing with her longer. I disagree on this and try to talk to her without upsetting her. She's very insecure.*"

"*Occasionally my husband will say something to her to help her understand.*"

And on the negative side:

"*[We deal with conflict] by her not talking to me and complaining to my husband instead of coming to me to talk it out.*"

"If they are minor, they are just ignored, if they can't be ignored, usually my husband will take over, and a huge blow-out occurs."

"My husband mediates, although he is EXTREMELY reluctant to get involved if he thinks it's going to make his parents angry, hurt, or upset. This is a challenge because his parents are VERY sensitive."

"My poor husband gets stuck in the middle. She is not open with me about her dislike for me - rather she voices her opinions to my husband. He gets stuck in the middle but will always take my side."

Screaming and yelling

There's not much positive to say about this method of handling conflict, but it sure is popular with some people. Bill Flatt, in his book, *Building a Healthy Family*,[v] talks about several causes of anger (the fuel behind screaming and yelling). Some people get angry because that's how they learned to respond to certain situations (perhaps from their parents) and what they have practiced in their own lives. People may get angry because of what they perceive as an injustice, either to themselves or to those they love. Some may feel frustrated, disappointed, hurt, inferior, or insecure, and act out in anger. Anger can build walls between people that separate them for many years. Hear the hurt in the comments we received from people who said this was how they handled conflict.

From one mother-in-law:

> *"They [conflicts] are not being resolved. She showers me with insults and bad words. Then she complains to her mother who yells at me some more. I think she hates me and I don't know why. I feel like I'm playing a game that I don't know the rules."*

And from a daughter-in-law:

> *"She screams and yells and then hangs up the phone and avoids me and never apologizes for anything."*

Cut-offs

During the course of this research, we've talked with hundreds of men and women about in-law relationships and, without a doubt, the saddest stories are those where a "cut-off" has occurred between the mother-in-law and the adult children, children-in-law, and grandchildren, particularly if the mother-in-law is genuinely unaware of what she has done. One woman told of a daughter-in-law who, for no reason known to her, stopped calling and then told the children they could not call their grandmother. When she called for their birthdays, she got the answering machine. She said:

> *"I have racked my brain and I honestly can't think of anything I have done. I wonder if they are embarrassed because of some financial difficulties they are having they don't want me to know about. But why would she keep me from my grandchildren?"*

And from another mother-in-law:

> *"My daughter-in-law resolves conflict with me by telling my son that I no longer can come over, call on the phone, see the grandchildren, and I am to be dead to them all."*

And from children-in-law:

> *"I am not speaking with her, period, so we have no conflict."* (Really??)

> *"I choose to avoid all contact save the absolutely necessary, superficial social niceties. She continually manipulates my husband, making her dislike of me*

his problem. I push back when necessary. I tend to lose regardless, but that is the pattern."

"I have had to cut off the relationship completely."

"I stay away from her, so there are not any more conflicts".

Susan Forward, in her book, *Toxic In-Laws: Loving Strategies to Protect Your Marriage*, differentiates toxic in-laws from in-laws who may simply be tacky or just not the in-laws you've always dreamed about. She defines toxic in-laws as those who create "genuine chaos" and not just discomfort.[vi]

Sometimes family members as well as friends can create "genuine chaos" in our lives. When that occurs, a cut-off may be considered. Too often, however, people make that decision hastily and in the heat of anger. Sometimes a person may take that action with manipulative intent, thinking, "If I do 'A' then he or she will do 'B'." Because people are highly unpredictable, the law of unintended consequences comes into play, and a cut-off may actually make the matter worse.

An intermediate step might be to call for a "moratorium on contact" for a period of time, as Forward calls it, for cooling off the negative impact and creating a strategy to improve the relationship. If that doesn't work, then the utmost care should be taken in deciding to completely cut off from a family member.

Family therapists tell us that cut-offs can be damaging from generation to generation. That is, if a person's *modus operandi* is to cut off from relationships rather than work through them, he (or she) actually stunts his abilities to resolve conflict effectively and, instead of working through interpersonal issues, simply begins cutting off more and more. Unfortunately, that same form of dealing with conflict modeled by parents may be passed down to the next generation. Adults who fail to resolve issues with **their** parents and instead create emotional or physical cut-offs may find **their own children** cutting off from them when they grow up, rather than resolving conflicts and staying connected.[vii] Often the physical and emotional cut-offs that I hear about usually started with a relatively fixable problem that just didn't get fixed and kept mushrooming.

If you are the one who has cut off, or if you have been cut off, consider reaching out, maybe first through a card or letter expressing sorrow over the loss of your relationship and a willingness to make the changes necessary to at least begin a dialogue. It may take time to rebuild trust and you may need to involve a trusted minister or counselor in the process. But isn't a relationship with those you love worth it?

Effective conflict resolution

Maybe some of the best wisdom we received regarded effective conflict resolution:

> *"We seldom have real conflicts, I think because we deflect potential problems by talking about them before they become conflicts."*

While deflecting conflicts before they arise may be the ideal, not everyone can manage that. So how do we get out of the mire of a conflict with our children-in-law? True conflict resolution usually requires some stretching out of our comfort zones. Or maybe just stretching outside of our bad habits. Do you know that when we are having a conflict with someone, research shows that we actually interpret what they say more negatively?[viii] Sometimes we do that because we quit listening before they quit talking, and so we assume we know what they are going to say. Or, since we know we already disagree with them in the first place and don't listen at all.

Listen

Therefore, the first order of business whenever a conflict arises is to listen to the other person. In counseling, I've found it's very helpful to have people actually practice "active and reflective listening" as discussed previously. I'm always amazed at how difficult repeating or paraphrasing what someone says can be at times. Remember from our previous chapter that we only hear about 50-75% of what is said to us. The other 25-50% of the time, we're thinking about what we want to say. If we are listening even less when we're having conflict, no wonder we get so frustrated. We aren't even hearing half of what's being said! But if you do listen to one another. . . well, here's what one daughter-in-law shared:

> *"My mother-in-law and I discuss it openly when something bothers one of us. We then discuss where each of us is coming from, which helps in mutual understanding & respect."*

Often, when we really listen to one another, we find that we want some of the same things. It's just our strategies that differ. If you can work your way back to something you can agree on (such as "We both want what is best for the children/grandchildren"), then maybe you can begin to take tiny steps forward to reach an agreement for how to accomplish that.

When we asked about being able to listen and/or consider others' opinions, 64% of the mothers-in-law said their children-in-law were able to consider other opinions. Sixty-two percent of the sons-in-law said their mothers-in-law would do the same. But only 44% of the daughters-in-law agreed their mothers-in-law were able to consider other opinions.

Interestingly, being able to consider another opinion was highly correlated with children-in-law who said they enjoyed good relationships with their mothers-in-law. Those children-in-law who said their mothers-in-law would not listen to other opinions were more likely to say they did not have good relationships with their mothers-in-law.

Bottom line, listening is important to resolving conflict and enjoying good in-law relationships.

Treat one another respectfully

Another element of conflict resolution is respect. I talk more about respect in the sons-in-law chapter, but when I say respect, I am not talking about respecting or agreeing with everything another person does. I'm talking about treating one another respectfully. One mother-in-law shared:

"I feel that while conflicts or differences may be painful, that we need to be respectful of one another and discuss them as they occur. Some conflict or differences may just be minor ones, however even these need to be cleared up. If I or the daughter-in-law do not know it bothers the other one, the conflict or differences will continue to happen, and this I am sure will build up over the years, and cause more damage in a single outburst then addressing it when it occurs. After all we both love the same person!"

A daughter-in-law seconded this:

"At times we agree to disagree. I try to be patient and flexible while standing firm. I try to be respectful of the fact that she is my elder and the mother of the husband I love."

Accepting one another for who s/he is

Contrary to popular belief, not every conflict has to be wrestled to the ground and agreed upon. OK, if you're trying to decide what color to paint a wall, that might be different. As a leader in a large organization, I noticed that sometimes when a person raised an objection to an issue, he might not want to change anything; he just wanted to be heard and acknowledged for his concerns. It's simply not in anyone's best interest to make a big deal out of every difference. Remember, "You need to pick the hill you're willing to die on." Not everything is worth arguing about, especially if a relationship hangs in the balance. A couple of children-in-law shared the following:

> *"We would have had fewer conflicts if I could have tolerated her quality of being so opinionated. If I could have accepted that she was entitled to express how she felt as long as she did not try to impose it on me."*

> *"I think if we would both be able to bite our tongues a little more it might be helpful. I am quite outspoken, and she is rather critical at times, so it can be a little difficult."*

Apology, forgiveness, and reconciliation

Often the words apology, forgiveness, and reconciliation get "mushed up" together, but in reality they are three separate actions. Apology is the act of recognizing a wrong and telling another person you are sorry. That may be accompanied by a request for forgiveness. Forgiveness begins with a decision to forgive, followed by a gradual letting go of the hurt, anger, and resentment felt towards another.[ix] Reconciliation refers to the restoring of a relationship.

Apology

When we asked the mothers-in-law in our survey if their children-in-law apologize when they are wrong, 44% said they do and 26% said they don't (the other 30% neither agreed nor disagreed). However, only 32% of the daughters-in-law said their mothers-in-law apologize and 49% said they don't. (Sons-in-law were 52% do, 27% don't.) Here's what some children-in-law said:

> *"It would help resolve our conflicts if she would give an outright apology for slandering me behind my back while I was right there and could hear her."*

> *"Apologizing to me for saying it was my fault my husband had an affair--admitting she was wrong to do that in front of my children."*

> *"Early on it would have been her EVER being able to admit that she might be wrong. Now, I just accept that as part of the whole fabulous person she is. She just can't imagine that she's wrong about anything or anyone. However, that confidence has taken her far."*

"I wish she would truly take responsibility for her inappropriate actions. She knows that she has messed up - yet she skirts around the responsibility issue and blames others instead of thinking how her actions contributed to the conflict."

"If she had actually acknowledged what she did wrong and apologized TO ME not my husband, along with telling the truth about what really happened instead of putting her spin on events to make herself look like the victim to the entire family."

As you hear in the above statements, lack of apology for a wrong committed can contribute to resentments building. Quite the reverse is true also. A sincere humble apology can help the injured party towards forgiveness.

Forgiveness

It has been said, "Only the injured man [or woman] can grant forgiveness."[x] If an uninsured driver backs into my car and I have a $200 deductible, I only have to forgive that person for $200 (and any other pain, suffering, and time expended in recovery). If my deductible is $500, then I have to forgive that amount. But if my deductible is zero and I experience no further inconvenience or problem from that event, there's really nothing to forgive because I'm not really out anything. I can only forgive for the part of me that is still hurt, or the gap between what we are "compensated" (so to speak) and whatever it would take for me to feel restored. In other words, all forgiveness is a "closing the gap."

How do we do that? Consider the following five-step process:[xi]

1) Accept the anger and sadness that come with the "injury."
2) Focus on the issue at hand, not the proverbial "everything but the kitchen sink" approach of blaming the current offense for everything else in life that has happened to you.
3) Work to empathize with the offender. This does NOT mean you agree with him or her, nor that whatever was done is OK. Just see if you can see what they did through their eyes.
4) Work to let go of the hurt and anger by deciding to think differently.
5) Tell the offender you forgive them.

Reconciliation

Reconciliation happens when the two parties, such as a mother-in-law and a daughter-in-law, have completed the processes of apology and forgiveness and are ready to restore their relationship to one of closeness again, or maybe begin their relationship anew and reach a level of trust and closeness they have not before experienced with one another. Not all forgiveness leads to reconciliation, but if at all possible, that should be the goal. Apology, forgiveness, and reconciliation take maturity, patience, and sometimes some hard emotional work. An email from a child-in-law captures the importance of reconciliation:

"I met my mother-in-law the day I started dating my husband and I immediately liked her. I felt that I had a lot in common with her and felt very accepted. However, when we got married, not everything went the way I would have preferred, and I started feeling insecure and upset. Over the first two years of my marriage, the hurt feelings continued to grow. I felt like she was more interested in my husband and her children than me. I did not feel like I fit in the family. She had done and said some things that hurt me. My husband is a conflict minimalist, so he kept encouraging me to "get over it." This was hard for me because I like to deal with things, and because I'm very verbal, talking is how I usually do that. For his sake, I kept quiet for two years, but finally I

couldn't take it anymore. It was too destructive. I didn't want to be mad at my mother-in-law. I loved and appreciated her and I knew she didn't mean to hurt my feelings. I worked very hard to forgive her and I finally approached her about the situation. I told her that I wanted to have a closer relationship, and that I was struggling with feeling like I didn't fit in the family. We talked for hours and she reassured me that she loved me as much as her children and explained some things about her family that helped me understand how to better interpret certain events and what to do to feel more comfortable. There are so many details I could write a lot about, but the main point was that that was the best phone call of my life. Everything changed at that moment (this happened just two months ago) and right now, I feel closer to her than I do to my mother. I am so thankful that I have the support and love of my mother-in-law and that I can trust her with myself. I no longer get offended because I trust her motives; if I misunderstand something she says, I feel comfortable talking to her about it. IT'S GREAT!"

For more information about forgiveness and reconciliation, check out the resources appendix.

Conflict is a part of life and can bring about a better understanding between people. Of course, it also holds the potential to drive people apart. If you've tried the above suggestions and still find yourself mired in conflict, seek help from a counselor who deals with extended family relationships. Sometimes, just having a third party to bounce ideas off of can help us sort through our thoughts better. Maybe you and your child-in-law can seek counseling together.

Whatever your struggles in this arena, seek to resolve them and restore. Isn't your relationship worth it?

---

[i] Helene S. Arnstein, *Between Mothers-in-Law and Daughters-in-Law* (New York: Dodd, Mead & Co., 1985), 29-49.

[ii] Evelyn Millis Duvall, *In-Laws: Pro and Con* (New York: Association Press, 1954),187-215.

[iii] Susan Forward, *Toxic In-Laws: Loving Strategies for Protecting Your Marriage* (New York: Quill, 2000), 6-7.

[iv] Bill Flatt, Building a Healthy Family (Nashville, TN: Gospel Advocate Company, 2001)…, 189

[v] Flatt, 186-88.

[vi] Forward, xi.

[vii] Gloria Call Horsley, *In-Laws: A Guide to Extended Family Therapy* (New York: John Wiley & Sons, 1996), 149-51.

[viii] Howard Markham, Scott Stanley, and Susan Blumbeg, *Fighting for Your Marriage*, (New York: John Wiley & Sons, 2001).

[ix] Everett Worthington, *Experiencing Forgiveness: Six Practical Sessions for Becoming a More Forgiving Christian* (Virginia Commonwealth University, 2006).

[x] Kristina Coop Gordon, Donald H. Baucom, and Douglas Snyder, "The Use of Forgiveness in Marital Therapy," in *Forgiveness: Theory, Research, and Practice*, ed. Michael McCullough, Kenneth Pargament, and Carl Thoresen (New York: The Guilford Press, 2000), 209.

[xi] Wanda M. Malcolm and Leslie S. Greenburg, "Forgiveness as a Process of Change in Individual psychotherapy, in *Forgiveness: Theory, Research, and Practice*, ed. Michael McCullough, Kenneth Pargament, and Carl Thoresen (New York: The Guilford Press, 2000), 179.

- 7 -

About Daughters-in-Law: Mothers-in-Law Speak Out

Let's face it, every relationship has two people in it (if not more). While it's nice to say that all problems are the other person's fault (and occasionally that may be the case), what each person does and says likely contributes, at least in part, to the problem. The survey found that those who consider themselves a good mother-in-law are more likely to say they have a good child-in-law, and those who feel they have a good mother-in-law consider themselves a good child-in-law, showing that the good in one may bring out the good in the other. But what do mothers-in-law think will impact their relationships with their daughters-in-law for the better? And how do you help your daughter-in-law to have a better relationship with you?

Cartoon copyrighted by Mark Parisi, printed with permission.

Your daughter-in-law is the one your son chose as his spouse, she may be the mother of your grandchildren, and, as such, she has an important role in your life. But that doesn't mean that she always has to like you, her mother-in-law. That certainly should be what you strive for, but realize that it doesn't always start nor end that way. At the very least you two have to get along and be able to be in the same room at the same time. Unless your daughter-in-law plans on getting rid of your son (her husband) just so she can permanently get away from you, you will be her mother-in-law for awhile. And remember, cut-offs are simply NOT the way to go. As the saying goes, you need to accept the things you cannot change and have the courage to change those things that you can.

A good first step to getting along is for both of you to consider your attitudes. The customer service industry often talks about having a positive attitude. In his "Give 'Em the Pickle" presentations (see http://www.giveemthepickle.com/), Bob Farrell of Farrell's Ice Cream talks about pasting a smile on your face no matter how you actually feel; actively working to outwardly be happy will eventually put you into a better mood. It may be a matter of what psychologists call *cognitive dissonance*, where the mind can't have two conflicting thoughts or emotions at the same time so tries to find a way to remove that conflict. The act of looking happy competes with the act of being mad, and since you are actively trying to look happy, that feeling then dominates and becomes your attitude (similar to the old saying about turning frowns upside-down). So, have a positive attitude; paste on a smile! If nothing else, your smile will make her wonder what you are up to, which could very well change her attitude! Your daughter-in-law may just do the same, because it may make her think that she did something to make you happy and you really don't hate her and everything she does after all.

Once you have a positive attitude, take the next step. As we've said in previous chapters, communication is KEY to any relationship. If someone doesn't know that they've upset you or how they've upset you, they cannot learn and actively take steps to improve the situation. When asked how conflicts are resolved, respondents said:

"Communication about [conflicts]. They are usually only misunderstandings."

"I feel that while conflicts or differences maybe be painful, that we need to be respectful of one another and discuss them as they occur. Some conflicts or differences may just be minor ones, however even

these need to be cleared up. If I or the daughter-in-law do not know it bothers the other one, the conflict or differences will continue to happen, and this I am sure will build up over the years, and cause more damage in a single outburst than addressing it when it occurs. After all, we both love the same person!"

Unfortunately, not all survey respondents can resolve their conflicts:

"We don't have conflicts any more. We have a very superficial relationship. We don't connect."

Once you are able to communicate, you can take steps to establish your boundaries (also discussed previously) and learn about hers:

"We haven't had any conflicts. I have a very strong sense of boundaries - mine and hers. I also remember what it was like to be a young bride and respect her need to find her own way."

Of course, if you are going to talk to someone, you also need to be able to hear what she says (that's half of communicating after all!), and actually hearing means you have to figure out how to be aware of your filters and not automatically shut down or get emotional when she starts talking. The goal of conversation about conflicts should simply be to resolve the situation and learn from the experience, not pin the blame. (Admittedly, pinning the blame may make you feel better briefly, but since you are in this relationship for the long haul, it ends up doing more harm than good.)

While attitude and conversation are big steps in improving your relationship, there are small things that your daughter-in-law can do, too, but you have to let her know that's what you want. As many mothers-in-law indicated, daughters-in-law doing things "just because" is a great place to start.

"Her calling to check on me - or just bringing the kids for a visit `just because`."

"Come over with my son to visit."

"Talk to me on the phone about personal things going on."

If you want your daughter-in-law to call or visit for no particular reason, suggest it to her. Tell her you'd like to see her (not your son, not the grandchildren, just her) or talk to her by herself to get to know her as a person; encourage her to call or visit for no real reason other than to talk. It'd be nice if she would also do things for you "just because" as well, like give you a little gift, tell you she saw an article that you might be interested in, etc., but if you want that, start by doing it for her. Get her something for one of her hobbies (e.g., quilting, scrapbooking, skydiving). BE SURE it's something fun for her (not a new dustrag, or vacuum cleaner, or cookbook [unless those are her hobbies])! And let her know you did it just because, with no strings attached other than that you'd like to have the kind of relationship with her where you do little nice things for each other. You will give her a surprise, showing you were thinking of her and paying attention to her (and her likes) without needing some holiday or other special occasion to do so. This might push her to do the same for you, especially if you point out to her that you enjoy putting your grandchildren's artwork on the fridge or collecting thimbles from around the world.

As mentioned before, advice can be a source of problems since it may be interpreted as criticism, even if you are just trying to give your daughter-in-law another perspective. Even with the best of intentions, you should likely hold your tongue unless asked. Tell her you are always willing to provide advice, but you realize that she needs to ask for it so that you don't overstep her boundaries. As one mother-in-law said, she would like her daughter-in-law to:

"Value my experience. Give 1 compliment a year."

Since you've likely been there before (young, starting a new family, with a mother-in-law), you know that she'll probably turn to her own mother or friends first since she's been listening to her/their advice for much longer than she's even known you. If she does ask for your guidance, realize that she may not actually do what you advise since asking for advice doesn't mean that you necessarily have to follow it. Don't be mad if she doesn't; she has to make her own decisions as she thinks best because that's what adults do and she is an adult. Be happy that she at least realized that you have more experience in life, in marriage, etc., than she does.

You may also want her to take a more active part in the family. Instead of sitting by herself during family get-togethers, try to involve your daughter-in-law in the conversation. She is now part of the family, and pretending otherwise will likely make her think that you don't want her there. The unannounced, "just because" visits could help here as well; on her next "just because" visit, let her know what is happening in the family so that she will be ready for the next family gathering. Perhaps you could tell her who has which political leanings, what topics are taboo and which are "safe", etc. Show that you realize that she is now – for better or worse – part of the family.

Mothers-in-law also revealed other things they wanted their daughters-in-law to do more or changes for the better, some of which may actually show the desire to improve the relationship with their daughter-in-law:

"I would love it if she would be more comfortable with me and less concerned with being p/c [politically correct]."

"If we lived closer."

"Spending more time together."

"Be more open and direct, with confidence that what she has to say is worth hearing."

"Get out more...have a wider exposure to life so that she can become more sophisticated."

A key to motivating change in the way people act is to reward them when they do something good (you probably learned that with your own child!), so let your daughter-in-law know that you appreciate her efforts. Even if she brings you a cake when you are on a diet, remember that it's the thought that counts. (And if she does bring you a cake, tell her to come over and help you eat it so you two can get to know each other better!)

The survey also asked mothers-in-law what their daughters-in-law could do that would cause a negative change in their relationship. The most common answer simply was criticism. Again, as we mentioned before, the balance of praise to criticism should be (at least) five praises for every criticism. Think about how you don't like to be criticized either, and let that be your guide. If you were in her position, would you REALLY have wanted your mother-in-law to criticize?

Most mothers-in-law realize that their daughter-in-law is there for her son and for any children they may have together, so many replied that the worst thing a daughter-in-law could do would be to cause harm to her husband or children. Additional comments included:

> *"If she stopped being welcoming to us in attitudes and in practice."*

"Not telling me about problems they are facing."

Regardless of changes that mothers-in-law might want in their daughters-in-law, they do realize their importance:

"[I value] the wonderful wife she is to my son and the great mothering she does for our two grandchildren."

"Peace knowing my son is loved."

Remember that there are two people in a mother-in-law/daughter-in-law relationship. If you have tried everything you and your son can think of to improve your relationship with your daughter-in-law, and moving far away and/or disconnecting the phone is not an option, accept her for who she is and how she is.

- 8 -

Sons-in-Law: Those Generally Jolly Gentleman

While sons-in-law made up only seven percent of those who responded to our survey, across the board they reported the best relationships with their mothers-in-law, enjoyed spending time with their mothers-in-law, and thought more highly of and more kindly towards their mothers-in-law than did daughters-in-law. Here's what one shared:

"From the moment I met her, I felt like I was already a member of the family. In many ways, she was more like my own mother, at least what I thought a mother should be."

And yet, if you think back to jokes and cartoons heard and seen, the vast majority of those come from the son-in-law's perspective (though this is changing). How many of us remember Rodney Dangerfield's famous one-liner, "Take my mother-in-law... Please!" Some of the earliest cartoons about mothers-in-law that we found in the Library of Congress depict the mother-in-law/son-in-law conflict.

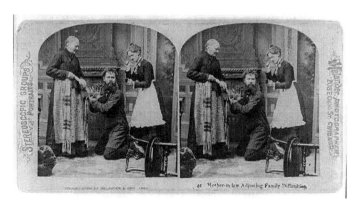

Some researchers have pondered, "Do cartoons reflect life or shape stereotypes?"[i] Others speculate that because men use humor more often than women to cope with or to diffuse difficult situations, the cartoons are simply a healthier way to express frustration and then to "let it go," so to speak. In fact, we caught glimpses of that from the sons-in-law in our survey. What's more, the men "out-humored" the women in "jest" (sorry, I couldn't resist) about every humor category, from "I like to think up funny jokes and stories" and "say amusing things" to asserting that humor is a good way to "master difficult situations" and "diffuse explosive situations."

The saving grace of humor

Undoubtedly, the funniest story we heard about mothers-in-law and sons-in-law came from our good friend Mark, who shared this yarn. Mark and his wife Karen, as well as Karen's sister, Brenda, and her husband Randy, were visiting Karen's mother in another city. Karen told Mark that her mother was redecorating and some of the sleeping arrangements had been changed. Mark stayed up late that night to finish a movie after everyone else had gone to bed. He said he made coffee and then tiptoed into the bedroom so he wouldn't wake Karen. Mark slipped out of his clothes and climbed into bed, whispered goodnight, and gave Karen an affectionate pat on the rump. Then his eyes popped open and he realized to his horror, "That's not Karen's rump!" Yep, you got it: it was his mother-in-law's! Mark said he fairly slithered out of the bed, picked up his shoes, and ran to the other bedroom where, he now remembered, Karen had told him earlier they would be sleeping.

The next morning, everyone else was up and sitting around the breakfast table when Mark walked into the room, but no one said a word about his "mistake" the previous night. Mark got some coffee and stood looking out the window for a few minutes trying to figure out what he should do. Should he just announce what he had done and see what the reactions were? Or, what if she had slept right through it? If he said something now, it might embarrass her and then he would feel like a heel. Mark said he couldn't think of one single other person he knew who had ever done anything remotely similar for him to draw any wisdom from.

While he was pondering his course of action, his mother-in-law broke the silence with, "Mark, last night was really special!" Now it was Mark's time to turn beet red when everyone laughed and wanted to hear the whole story again. Mark said he already enjoyed a great relationship with his mother-in-law,

but her handling of that experience cemented his love
and admiration for her and for her sense of humor!

"SORRY I'M LATE – I WAS HELD UP AT THE
OFFICE. HAS YOUR MOTHER LEFT YET?"

From www.CartoonStock.com, used with permission.

Dr. Joel Goodman, founder of The HUMOR Project, Inc. in Saratoga Springs, New York, has been taking humor seriously for over 30 years. The HUMOR Project, the first organization of its kind to focus full-time on the positive power of humor, strives to "help people get more smileage out of their lives and jobs by applying the practical, positive power of humor and creativity."

Why is humor important? Dr. Goodman has many reasons[ii], among them:

1. **The funny line and the bottom line intersect!** In a survey of 737 CEOs, over 98% of them indicated they would much rather hire somebody with a good sense of humor than somebody without one. You can take your job seriously... and yourself lightly!

2. **Jest for the health of it!** Laughter enhances respiration and circulation, oxygenates the blood, suppresses the stress-related hormones in the brain, and activates the immune system. Indeed, laughter is the jest medicine!

3. **Humor as an antidote to stress:** Humor can help us to move from a "grin and bear it" mentality to a "grin and share it" orientation. By using humor, you can prevent a "hardening

of the attitudes," which can help you add years to your life and life to your years.

4. **"A smile is the shortest distance between two people,"** according to Victor Borge. Humor can be a magnet to attract people, to build positive working relationships, and to improve morale and teamwork.

5. **The HAHA-AHA connection:** There definitely is a connection between humor and creativity. Humor can jump-start your creativity and give you the energy to think (and laugh) outside the box!

6. **The laughing-learning link:** Humor can be a powerful (and delightful) way to capture and maintain attention and free up tension...which means that retention increases!

7. **Your Resilience Quotient:** Norman Cousins' best-selling book, *Anatomy of an Illness*, certainly opened up many people's eyes to the notion of "S/He who laughs lasts." With humor, you can build resilience and get more smileage out of your life and work.

8. **Humor as a saving (and amusing) grace for the planet:** As our world gets proverbially smaller all the time, humor could help build

important bridges between countries and cultures. As Erma Bombeck once said, "When humor goes, there goes civilization!"

It's unclear if the men in our survey were thinking exactly along those lines when they answered, but not only did the men place greater value on humor, they also tended to have more positive opinions and expectations in every category about their mothers-in-law than women:

	son-in-law	daughter-in-law
My mother-in-law gives unsolicited praise	61%	54%
My mother-in-law respects the boundaries of our marriage	69%	55%
My mother-in-law apologizes when she is wrong	52%	32%
My mother-in-law will consider other opinions	61%	44%
My mother-in-law has a good sense of humor	73%	54%

Note: Percent who indicated "Yes."

Numerous research studies outline the strong connection between thoughts and feelings. As we mentioned in the previous chapter, the way we think can actually change the way we feel. And if we feel more positively about a person or situation, we are more apt to give him or her the benefit of the doubt. For the men in our survey, their upbeat opinions and expectations seemed to translate into more positive interactions with their mothers-in-law as shown in the following:

	son-in-law	daughter-in-law
I can discuss difficult problems with my mother-in-law	44%	30%
I can forgive my mother-in-law for past hurts	68%	58%
I enjoy spending time with my mother-in-law	68%	48%
I have a good relationship with my mother-in-law	75%	56%

Note: Percent who indicated "Yes."

Not nirvana, but workable

While the men in our survey boasted better overall relationships with their mothers-in-law, they also indicated some of the same issues and problems shared by the daughters-in-law: no respect for boundaries, criticizing the wife/daughter, and interfering with disciplining the children, as well as more unique issues such as drug use, creating discord, borrowing money and not paying it back, calling too often, calling or visiting when the family is busy, criticizing, and giving her opinion too freely. About five percent of the men indicated they handled this conflict with their mothers-in-law by avoiding certain subjects or avoiding the mother-in-law all together. Less than ten percent said their mothers-in-law were not willing to listen, not willing to discuss the problem in a reasonable manner, nor resolve the conflict amicably. Almost thirty percent of the men indicated they had *no conflict* with their mothers-in-law. The vast majority stated they resolved problems together effectively, mainly by talking it out. Here's what they said:

"We talk things out if we have a disagreement and we can agree to disagree."

"We talk them out and listen to each other."

"We talk about them when they come up. Usually she takes advice well and listens to me."

"We forgive and forget."

"Respect one another; if you have any differences you must talk them through resolution. While dating, get to know your mother-in-law just as well. One must remember that one is marrying into a family, not just that one person."

Sons-in-law are easier?

Over the course of the past two years, whenever I (Leanne) have been involved in a discussion about sons-in-law and daughters-in-law, at least one mother-in-law states, "Sons-in-law are much easier." These women are often quick to state they love their daughters-in-law, but find the relationships with their sons-in-law less stressful and conflicted. Unless the son-in-law is abusive, addicted, chronically unemployed, or unfaithful, most women with both sons- and daughters-in-law agree the mother-in-law/son-in-law relationship seems more relaxed.

Some suggest the disparity exists because of an innate rivalry between the two women, whereas that competition doesn't exist between the son-in-law and the mother-in-law. Others have suggested that maybe since there's a lower expectation for close communication and relationship between the son-in-law and the mother-in-law, feelings are less apt to get hurt and the two can interact more naturally. Clearly this phenomenon calls for further research.

If you suffer a poor relationship with your son-in-law and can't identify with this chapter, please take a look at the communication and conflict resolution chapters to see if that may offer some insight. If you are dealing with a son-in-law who is abusive, addicted, chronically unemployed or unfaithful, even if neither he nor your daughter wants to seek counseling, you may find ways to help them, as well as ways for you to cope, by seeking counseling for yourself with a family therapist experienced in dealing with extended family relationships. Check out our Resources section.

What struck me as I read the comments from the men in our survey was the clear affection and admiration many of them showed for their mothers-in-law. When we asked what their mothers-in-law contributed to their lives, they answered with terms like acceptance, support, love, caring, encouragement, consideration, godly example, respect, nurturing, care and love of grandchildren, optimism, compassion, sense of humor, and the list went on and on. Others wrote more:

> *"I value her willingness to be part of our life by visiting regularly and contributing to running our family life when here. Letting my wife and I go away for our anniversary every year may be the best gift she could give us because it supports our marriage. She really is an important part of our family and we wish she would live closer to us. I think I am very lucky to have her as a mother-in-law. I can't think of a way she could be any better for us and our family."*

> *"I value her total support of me and my wife; her willingness to let my wife and me work out our difficult problems without getting in the middle of them; her ability to not take sides when my wife and I are having difficult times; her unconditional support and love."*

> *"I wish she could be more involved in our family life."*

(From a son-in-law whose mother-in-law is deceased) *"I appreciated the mutual respect and appreciation we had for one another. My mother-in-law and I were more like son and mother and there was respect and caring, acceptance and sharing. There was incredible love between my mother-in-law and me."*

Love and respect: A final word

Emerson E. Eggerichs, in his book *Love and Respect*,[iii] shares his "discovery" that men and women are different. "Well, duh", you might say, "I knew that." Now before I go one step farther, for those of you who say, "Now wait a minute, you just can't make those kinds of sweeping statements about anything other than physical differences," I admit that not *all men* and not *all women* fall into neat little categories. But what Eggerichs says bears hearing and it relates directly to your relationship with your son-in-law.

Eggerichs tells how women seek love in relationships. Not just male/female relationships but in all relationships, with our friends, maybe even with our acquaintances. Men need love, for sure, but what they need even more, Eggerichs posits, is respect. Yes, women need respect too, but men seem to need that in greater portions. Men need love, but women seem to thrive on love. As women, we're familiar with using love words. That's our language and we know it well. But many (dare I say, *most?*) men don't always speak the language of love. Eggerichs says the language men speak is "respect language."

We often talk about "unconditional love" as the gold standard for relationships. But we rarely talk about "unconditional respect." Instead, we talk about respect as being something that must be earned, especially in our close relationships. I'm familiar with this concept of unconditional respect from my career in the military. The very first day of my officer training I was told I would respect the position of senior officers. I learned throughout my Navy career that I didn't like some of those people very much, but I said, "Aye, aye, Sir," and *treated them respectfully.* I respected the rank they had attained and I honored them as my superiors. Liking them played little role in how I was expected to treat them.

Now that's an extreme example, but one that may apply. You may not like your son-in-law very much, but there's nothing that prevents you from offering him unconditional respect because, you see, it's not based on how you *feel* about him. It's based on how you decide to *treat* him. Wouldn't it be worth giving unconditional respect a try to help heal a broken relationship? And what if you *do* like him? What if you even *love* him? Wouldn't it be worth giving it a try to make a good relationship even better?

Get a sheet of paper and make a list of ten things you like and respect about your son-in-law. Maybe he's good with computers – one of the many things my son-in-law does with ease – or maybe he's a handyman, a good and loving father to your grandchildren, a financial wizard, a good basketball player, a godly man, a great golfer, well, you get the idea. Maybe he usually thanks you for meals you fix for him or for rides to get his car fixed, maybe he comes and unplugs your toilet whenever you call, maybe he takes your dog to the vet.

Some of you might have to think a little harder. Maybe he's held this job for two months, been clean and sober for four weeks, hasn't been arrested for a year, or showed up at the hospital right before or after his first child was born. Just like Eggerichs suggests a wife do for a husband, you can do for a son-in-law (or any other man in the family). Tell him, "I have respect for you for," and then tell him 2-3 things on your list. Remember the 5-to-1-praise rule I discussed earlier? Be sincere and tell him often. Just like women need to hear love words, men need to hear respect words. For more information, I strongly suggest you read the book *Love and Respect*. It might just change many of your relationships for the better!

From our study, sons-in-law seem to be predisposed to good relationships with their mothers-in-law. While conflicts exist, just like they do with daughters-in-law, the men in our survey indicated they often approach in-law difficulties with a sense of humor or a desire for humor to diffuse the conflict. Many feel a deep sense of connection with their mothers-in-law. With all those positives, mothers-in-law can expect to enjoy good relationships with their sons-in-law. Treating them with respect can go a long way in cementing this bond.

---

[i] Christina Nuta, "Do cartoons reflect reality or are they a mere joke?" written for *Famous Why*, http://articles.famouswhy.com/do_cartoons_reflect_reality_or_are_they_a_mere_joke_/, accessed April 5, 2008.

[ii] Joel Goodman, The HUMOR Project, Inc., http://www.humorproject.com/about/humorwise.php , accessed April 19, 2008. This originally appeared in *Laughing Matters* magazine, edited by Joel Goodman, and also appears in the *2008 Humor Sourcebook,* published by The HUMOR Project, 480 Broadway, Suite 210, Saratoga Springs, NY 12866 (518-587-8770).

[iii] Emerson E. Eggerichs, *Love and Respect* (Nashville, TN: Thomas Nelson, 2004).

- 9 -

The Grandmothering Mother-in-law

When a new life enters this world, it represents a time of change for everyone involved, and that includes the mother-in-law, who – in the blink of an eye – gets a new title. "Grandmother." I (Leanne) just couldn't stop saying that word after my daughter called me one autumn evening 11 years ago and said, "Hey, Mom, how would you like to be a grandmother?" Though she and my son-in-law had been married for five years, they were still paying off law school loans and hadn't exactly planned on a child quite that soon, but they were happy and I was happy. Actually, I was over the moon! When I got off the phone, I sat in a daze for a few minutes. Grandmother, imagine that? I couldn't wait to call all my friends and tell them! But, "Unfortunately," as one writer lamented, "an operator's license doesn't come along with the new titles."[i] Just like you might have asked yourself earlier, "What's a mother-in-law?" you might be asking yourself now, "What's a grandmother?"

It doesn't take a genius to discern that this generation of grandmothers isn't exactly like those say, 40-50 years ago. My grandmother was over 70 when I was born and I remember her as a quiet, gentle woman, sitting in her rocking chair, singing and telling stories. Some of my friends remember grandmothers who baked cookies, worked on the farm, canned and preserved, and made them beautiful dresses. When I look around at grandmothers I know today, I see college professors, doctors, Naval officers, realtors, motorcycle-riders, teachers, and nurses, as well as homemakers. Some grandmothers may not work for pay, but they work full time for volunteer organizations or they travel to distant lands, fulfilling dreams of earlier years. Still other grandmothers babysit on a regular basis because both parents work and Grandma is able, willing, and often happy to play that important role in her grandchildren's lives.

My cousin Mary Lynn has four sons, so when she became grandmother to a little girl, she quit working at a preschool she helped start so she could keep Shelby during the day. Regardless of your life situation, you have choices about the grandparent role you want to play and the family heritage you want to share with these precious little people.

Styles of grandparenting
Researchers have identified six general grandparenting styles:[ii]

1. **The grandchildren take center stage:** These folks put their grandparent role foremost in their lives, and even close friends and other activities take a backseat.

2. **Wise and valued elder:** These grandparents concentrate on assuming the role of wise and valued advisor and passing on skills and traditions to their grandchildren.

3. **Immortality through their grandchildren:** These grandparents see their grandchildren as providing a means to immortality through the continuity of family.

4. **Reliving their own past:** These grandparents enjoy experiencing everything in their grandchildren's lives – from piano recitals to Cub Scouts – and remembering when they and/or their own children were the same ages as their grandchildren.

5. **Spoiling:** These grandparents look forward to spoiling their grandchildren and are seen as more lenient than they were with their own children.

6. **Reluctant:** These grandparents have difficulty with the transition to grandparenthood and may think they are "too young to be grandparents." One author says this tendency first shows up in what they want to be called by their grandchildren, sometimes wanting to be called by their first names.[iii]

While grandparents may actually exhibit all the above styles at one time or another, the list may provide a useful tool for you to begin thinking about your own grandparenting style as well as what kind of influence you want to have and the legacy you want to leave for your grandchildren.

The birth and the days following

Depending on whether you are the maternal or paternal grandmother, the rules of the upcoming game might be a bit different, but not necessarily better or worse. When it's time for the much-anticipated grandchild to arrive, women often want their mothers with or near them, but not necessarily their mothers-in-law unless the relationship is extremely close. My daughter, who is a very private person, surprised me by wanting me in the delivery room. My daughter-in-law, on the other hand, whose mother lives on the opposite coast and wasn't able to get to town in time for the birth, only wanted her husband (my son) and her best friend with her. As much as possible, clarify your role, but if you are going to assume anything, assume you will not be in the delivery room. As a mother-in-law, the best advice here is to follow the wishes of your adult child and child-in-law, and always defer to the wishes of your daughter or daughter-in-law if there's a disparity.

If you have given birth yourself, you know labor is a high stress event, and unless you can in some way comfort, coach, or help directly in the process, you should probably stay in the waiting room and read a magazine. If there are older children, you can be very helpful with their care, either at home or at the hospital. The whole process can be very scary to a child who sees his or her mother in pain and then rushed to the hospital. I once heard a story about a little boy who told his daddy that he was crying because he thought his mother was going to die! Wise, knowledgeable grandmothers can help allay children's fears and help them to understand what's happening as best they can in children's terms. Bottom line, discuss the birth with your adult child and child-in-law way ahead of time and make sure there are no misunderstandings, which can lead to high drama and/or hurt feelings on the big day.

If you are a mother-in-law to a daughter-in-law who has said she would like for both you and her mother to visit during the first few weeks, ask her when she would like for you to be there, first or last (e.g. for the birth and for a week or two following? Or would she rather have her mother with her for the first week or two and then have you help after that?) If the daughter-in-law's mother is unable to be there for the birth or in the few weeks following the birth, it would be unwise for the mother-in-law to *assume* that she should step into the gap without discussing this thoroughly with her daughter-in-law. You may have the best of intentions, you may even be able to help her in ways neither of you have dreamed of, but especially during this time – I'll repeat myself – *do not assume anything.*

If a daughter-in-law doesn't readily accept her mother-in-law's help, there could be several reasons and some of them in no way reflect a poor mother-in-law/daughter-in-law relationship. For example, one daughter-in-law I spoke with tearfully shared that her mother could not financially manage the trip to be with her for the birth, and even though she assured her mother she understood, her mother still felt both sad and guilty. When the mother-in-law talked to her daughter-in-law about coming to help, the daughter-in-law said she felt torn:

"I would love to have the extra help and support, because I genuinely love my mother-in-law and I know she would like to be with us. But I'm afraid if she comes that will make my Mom feel even worse about not being able to be here for the birth of her first grandchild. It's not that I don't want my mother-in-law; I just don't want to hurt my Mom and I don't know what to do."

Try to be sensitive to these kinds of underlying issues and loyalties, and make it a point to place as few demands and inject as little stress into the situation as possible. If your mother-in-law/daughter-in-law relationship is rocky, now is not the time to be the proverbial "bull in the china shop."

Think about the long-term relationship, not just about the birth. If you are not in the delivery room, maybe you can still be at the hospital. If you're not at the hospital, maybe you can come to see your grandchild the following day. If you live out of town, maybe you can ask for a phone call and an email photo. Maybe you will have to wait a few days, weeks, or months to hold that precious little package. Instead of dwelling on what you don't have, consider the blessing of a grandchild that you do have and love from a distance until you can be there. Some of that could go a long way in helping repair any rough spots.

The birth of a child seems to increase overall interactions and triggers changes in the dynamics of the mother-in-law/child-in-law relationship.[iv] One writer indicates the mother-in-law/child-in-law relationship may actually return to the "storming" stage that we discussed in Chapter 3, where conflicts increase for a period of time as a new "norm" is being established. "What one in-law perceives as offering help, another perceives as intrusion",[v] especially during the first few days or weeks the new family is at home.

However, research suggests that mothers and daughters may actually grow closer following the birth of a grandchild in that the relationship changes from a "mother-child" to a "mother-mother" relationship. (Married daughters with children report more contact, telephonically and in person, with their mothers than childless daughters, regardless of the distance between them.)[vi] Because of those dynamics, it may be wise for your daughter-in-law's mother to be the one to help first since your daughter-in-law has a longer history with her and likely will view her mother's suggestions in a better light. However, if you pull first duty, at least be aware of the "storming" tendency, and guard against any unsolicited advice or criticism.

In some instances, the birth of a new grandchild could draw the mother-in-law and daughter-in-law closer. A woman I met at a conference a few months ago told me that in the early years of her marriage, she hadn't gotten along very well with her mother-in-law. She perceived her mother-in-law as a bit bossy and critical. But, she said, "When I was in the hospital holding my little son in my arms for the first time, it struck me: 'I'm going to be a mother-in-law to this child's wife some day!' And after that, I looked at my own mother-in-law in a whole different light."

In one of the most bittersweet stories told us, one daughter-in-law shared:

"Four years ago, I gave birth (at 27 weeks) to a stillborn son. The morning after coming home from the hospital, I had an emotional break down while getting dressed when I realized that maternity clothes were too big, and my regular clothes were too small. My mother-in-law came into my bedroom and asked what was wrong, so I blubbered the problem out. She looked down at herself, and said, this outfit would look perfect on you, and she literally took the clothes off her back and dressed me in them!!!! And you know what? They did look great on me, and I was able to take a deep breath and face one more day. I will NEVER EVER forget that. A moment that will always be treasured in my heart."

My mother's sister, who was a nurse, came to stay with me after my daughter was born. She told me right off the bat that she was there to take care of me and the house so that I could be free to take care of my new baby. Regardless of when you help, that still seems like valuable advice to follow. My daughter even mentioned that her fear, when I came to help after the birth of her first child, was that I would "take over" care of the newborn. She was happy to know what her wise great-aunt had taught me so many years before.

Are grandmothers good for children or bad for children?

Dr. Evelyn Duvall, in *In-Laws: Pro and Con*, indicated several sources that showed grandmothers were bad for grandchildren! One source stated that they attempted to re-live their own parenting days, clinging to the child and fighting the mother for the child's affection.[vii] From another source, she cites "10 Mistakes Grandparents Make":[viii]

1. Too much baby talk
2. Picking up baby when he cries
3. Feeding the child without parents' consent
4. Paying the child to do his duty
5. Too many gifts
6. Challenging a parent's decision
7. Too much pampering
8. Punishing the child without parental consent
9. Encouraging a child to outwit his parents
10. Failing to share their accumulated wealth

Our survey participants echoed some of those same issues.

Undermining values and discipline

It's important that mothers-in-law remember they are their children's parents NOT their grandchildren's parents.

"[I would like my mother-in-law to stop] interfering in the way my husband and I raise our children. We have 5 kids and we are Christian. She is not a Christian; she says she is, but she believes in magic and other weird stuff and tries to tell our kids about them."

"She does not hold my children accountable for rules and makes excuses for them because it's grandma's house."

"[I would like for her to] respect me and my husband's wishes on how to take care of our son. She will do this if my husband talks to her before a visit. It's like we have to remind her every time."

"[I would like to be able] to express preferences/rules without `feelings getting hurt.` For example, my children do not go to my mother-in-law's house because she smokes in her home; that hurts her feelings instead of considering the damage it does to her grandchildren."

"[I would like it] if she would realize that I am the parent now, and these are my children, not just her grandchildren entrusted to my care."

"[I would like her to stop] being the parent to her grandchildren (our children) while we are present."

"[I would like her to stop] undermining my authority by not allowing me to be the parent/disciplinarian to my own children."

My cousin Mary Lynn (daytime babysitter for her 5 year-old granddaughter Shelby Lynn) said:

"When I learned that our son, Scott, and daughter-in-law, Terri, were expecting our first grandchild, I was excited to say the least and immediately decided that I would quit my job and be a full time "Granmommy" (if asked). Several weeks later when Terri mentioned that she needed help with locating child care, I simply said, "My child care is available". We were all very happy with the plan. However, being a "thinker" I knew it would be a tremendous responsibility to have a little one to care for <u>and</u> keep the family congenial with all the many decisions that would emerge. I had heard friends tell horror stories of how children and in-laws could face

lots of friction after grandchildren arrived. I did not want that to happen. To, hopefully, avoid it I told myself from the beginning that this would <u>not</u> be my child; important decisions would be made by parents and I would always try to comply."

Undermining parents' authority will ultimately cause problems. If children are encouraged to disobey their parents' rules by the grandmother, she is, in effect, teaching those children to disobey authority, which could have far-reaching impact. If the children are in her care in her home, the rules that parents set must stand, including bedtimes, food choices, etc. Sometimes, parents will make allowances for special occasions when grandparents come to visit or children visit grandparents in their homes, but the child must know that what the parents say always trumps the grandparent.

When should a grandmother step in and take action? If there are clear and compelling signs of physical abuse or sexual abuse, decisive action must be taken immediately. Most state Departments of Children Services operate a 24-hour hotline where anonymous reports are accepted. If a grandmother believes her grandchild is being verbally or emotionally abused, she can also report that behavior anonymously.

However, most disciplinary concerns that grandmothers have fall short of the above categories. In those cases, she should speak with one or both of the parents. There appears to be some debate over who the mother-in-law/grandmother should approach. One side states she should speak directly with the child or child-in-law with whom she has a concern; the other side opts for the mother-in-law/grandmother to speak directly with both adult child and child-in-law so everything is open and above-board. The direction each grandparent takes is highly dependent on the relationship she has developed with her adult child and child-in-law. Regardless of the path to get there, the clear message must be what is best for the child, rather than which parenting/grandparenting style "wins."[ix]

***Too much stuff!* (The over-indulgence syndrome)**

One of the more common complaints in almost every mother-in-law reference deals with "stuff." Maybe it should be a rule that before grandparents can give a grandchild another toy, they have to go to the grandchild's house and clean up the toy clutter for a week! That might give a greater appreciation of what some young parents deal with everyday. One young mother told us:

> *"[My mother-in-law overwhelms] the kids with too many presents. I appreciate that these are her only grandchildren and she's very enthusiastic, but she goes so overboard at Christmas and birthdays (lots of knick-knack type stuff that just clutters their bedrooms) that it gets to the point where they don't appreciate it and I fear for them getting spoiled. My eldest is 10 and had confided that she feels overwhelmed by it and prefers my mother's gift-giving style of one very meaningful gift. My husband gets so overwhelmed by clutter that it has actually caused marital tension, and I finally had to point out to him that so much of the kids' stuff that's lying around is from his mother, and if he was going to let it stress him out so much he needed to address it with her."*

The gift-giving motivation for most grandparents is the genuine desire to see the child's excitement as they open the gift or try on the new clothes, etc. However, moderation must rule. Note in the above quote that not only do the excess gifts cause clutter, they also lead to marital tension! Discuss gifts with your grandchildren's parents and ask what they believe would be reasonable in terms of dollar amount, number of gifts, and type of gifts. Some grandparents limit their gifts to a certain dollar amount. Others limit gift-giving to one gift and one book per occasion (Christmas, birthday, etc.). Online "wish lists" can be enormously helpful in corralling the types of gifts children receive. Parents can complete the lists for younger children and monitor them for older children, and grandparents have ready access to gift ideas.

A couple of words of caution about gifts. First, gifts should be given from the heart and not for any ulterior motive, such as "encouraging" a grandchild to love one grandmother better than another. Grandmothers may, consciously or unconsciously, compete for the grandchildren's affections by seeing who can buy and give the biggest or the most expensive gifts. At best, this can lead to frustration. At worst, it can lead to hurt feelings and resentment by the other grandmother and the child-in-law. Remember, what grandchildren really respond to is genuine affection and time a grandmother spends with her grandchild.[x] (And research suggests that families tend to draw closer when the two grandmothers form a close alliance with one another instead of against one another.)

Second, a grandmother should make every effort to treat every grandchild equitably, and that includes gift-giving. It's virtually impossible to treat grandchildren exactly equally because each has different needs. In Gary Chapman's *The Five Love Languages*, he tells us that each of us has a certain "love language" that communicates or resonates love best to us. The five "languages" include:

1. Words of affirmation
2. Gifts and cards
3. Acts of service
4. Quality time
5. Physical touch

We tend to "speak" to others in the love language we ourselves enjoy. I am a "words of affirmation" person. Nothing tells me I'm loved better than a well-placed compliment. I like flowers, cards, and gifts OK, but a compliment wins out any day for me. So when I want to show love, I tend to tell others how proud I am of their accomplishments, or how much they mean to me.

That probably works well for others who respond best to "words of affirmation." The key, however, is finding and learning to speak love in another's love language. In other words, giving "stuff" might not be speaking the love you want to convey to your grandchild.

My 6-year-old granddaughter is a hugger. When I sit on the sofa, she's right there with me hugging me and snuggling up next to me. She also likes cards (homemade ones are fine), so I would say her primary love language is either physical touch or gifts and cards. My 10-year-old grandson probably responds best to quality time. He just likes for me to be nearby watching him play video games. He especially likes to ride four-wheelers with his other grandmother when they tour the perimeter of her "ranch" when he visits her. Both grandchildren like gifts, but if I only relied on that, I could be missing out on conveying to them my love in a way that effectively communicates with each one. What's your grandchild's love language?

Not praising, or worse

When we asked our survey participants about what change they would like their mothers-in-law to make, here's what they said:

"I would like my mother-in-law to stop telling my daughter that she is too fat. She hasn't even finished growing yet and I don't think this should be an issue. There are too many kids out there already with

eating disorders and I don't want [her grandmother's] opinion to lead to one for my daughter."

"I want my mother-in-law to stop being negative about her grandchildren."

"I would love for her to praise the grandchildren and overlook their mistakes."

"Tell the grandchildren directly how wonderful they are."

Children are more motivated by praise than by criticism. If you use the 5 to 1 rule discussed before, you may earn the right to give constructive criticism. Cutting remarks will NOT motivate change and WILL crush a child's innocent love.

"I wish my mother-in-law would stop talking about things she has done with specific grandchildren in front of the other grandchildren."

"I wish she would stop taking the side of the other grandchildren over mine."

"I wish my mother-in-law placed the same importance on my children as she places on her

daughter's children - or the grandchildren of her new husband (very involved with all of these, only ignores mine)."

"I wish my mother-in-law would start loving my children (her grandchildren), and treat them in a similar manner as she does her other grandchildren."

The need for fairness, even-handedness, and equitable treatment make a showing here. Comparing grandchildren, treating grandchildren differently from one family or the other, or talking ill about one grandchild (or child, child-in-law, other family member, etc.) to another grandchild is NEVER appropriate. Regardless of the mother-in-law's relationship with her adult child or child-in-law, a mother-in-law must look past that and love her grandchildren. They are innocent and they desperately want to be loved.

Disinterest in grandchildren

Even in Duvall's in-law book, published in the 1950s, the issue of mothers-in-law's "disinterest" in relatives rates discussion. Many times this problem has deep roots. Conflicts with children-in-law and their families can create distances in relationships that are not easily repaired, and so some mothers-in-law opt for maintaining an emotional distance or even cutting off the relationships with her adult child, child-in-law, and grandchildren entirely. Other times, a mother-in-law's job or care of aging parents or other family members can leave her little time to grandparent. Still others, too involved in their own pursuits and activities, choose not to make the time for grandparenting. Here's what some of our survey respondents said. You may not agree with them all, but they may give you some ideas or insight into your own grandmothering.

> *"...She loved the idea of having grandchildren (we had the only ones) but she really never made any effort to let them or us know that they were considered to be very special to her."*

> *"[I would like my mother-in-law to] spend more time with her grandchildren. But I know (and accept) that she is tired and busy (writing books). We spend good time together, I just wish it were more often, and with just the grandchildren."*

> *"[I wish she] initiated spending more time with her grandchildren."*

"*[I would like] more communication initiated from her, especially to her grandchildren and for special occasions, i.e. birthdays, holidays.*"

"*[I wish she would show] any sign of interest in her grandchildren.*"

"*[I wish she would be] willing to babysit and be with her grandchildren.*"

"*[I wish she would] show a genuine interest in my children without a seeming agenda behind her actions.*"

"*[I wish she would] spend more quality time with grandchildren.*"

"*[A good mother-in-law/child-in-law relationship is one where she would be] willing to take grandchildren for a day or to come to events of kids, not try to pry info out of daughter-in-law, not make judgments. Teach grandkids things, love them, be interested in them.*"

Children need grandparents

In the normal course of life events, children need their grandparents for several reasons beyond the unconditional love they give.

Grandparents can provide a historical perspective on life, culture and family

My 95-year old mother has been a vast source of information to her grandchildren and great-grandchildren. Not only can she tell them from first-hand experience about their great-great grandparents and other people who make up their family heritage, but she can also relate stories to them about growing up on a farm, riding a horse to school, chopping cotton, and de-bugging potato plants when she was growing up, and how very different daily life was back then. When she tells them her favorite childhood games and pastimes, such as swinging, playing dolls, and playing church with her friends, and what they studied in school, they see how children then and now maybe aren't that different after all. It gives them a guided-tour of the past while providing them with continuity into their own lives.

Cartoon copyrighted by Mark Parisi, printed with permission.

One mother said:

"I think being a grandparent is very important to the emotional well being of my children as it gives them a sense of belonging to something larger, an extended family. Memories are made with grandparents."

Another young mother said:

*"She has allowed her home to be a `home` for my kids.
My husband is in the military and we move around a
lot. My mother-in-law has been very open with her
home and really wants my kids to visit. This gives
them a sense of being from somewhere."*

Grandparents are a great source of babysitting and other help with the children

Grandparents can step in and help with babysitting, either on a daily basis like my cousin Mary Lynn has done, or for other periods of time. One woman told us she babysits one day each week so her daughter-in-law can have a day to go grocery shopping without whining toddlers, out to lunch with a friend, or just spend a quiet day at home. Some grandparents babysit so their child and child-in-law can go out for weekly date nights, or when parents take business trips or (usually much-needed) vacations. One mother said:

*"[I appreciate my mother-in-law's] willingness to
babysit for us when we go on yearly vacations
alone."*

Knowing that the children are in the loving and capable care of a grandparent can provide reassurance for parents and allow them to relax and enjoy their time away from the children. As one young mother wrote about their night out without their baby daughter:

> *"What made the dinner even better was the fact that it was spent in the company of some of my favorite people, having great conversation and also it helped me to remember what it feels like to be without Adelaide. Not to say that I don't love being with her. I do! But it was good to sit, alone, with no one pulling on me. It was nice to wear clean clothes and have them stay that way--all night! It was wonderful to talk to adults and be able to give them my full attention. And it was really nice to be able to do all these things without having to worry about Adelaide at all because she was home with Gram!"*

Enrich children's lives

Time with grandparents is different from being with parents, but has a familiar feel to it for grandchildren. It also gives them an unhurried place to experience life and to be loved. When asked, here's what some eight-year olds said about grandparents:[xi]

"When they take us for walks, they slow down past things like pretty leaves and caterpillars."

"They show us and talk to us about the color of the flowers and also why we shouldn't step on 'cracks'."

"They don't say, 'Hurry up'."

"They have to answer questions like 'Why isn't God married?' and 'How come dogs chase cats?'"

"When they read to us, they don't skip. They don't mind if we ask for the same story over again."

"Everybody should try to have a grandmother, especially if you don't have television, because they are the only grown-ups who like to spend time with us."

"They know we should have snack-time before bedtime and they say prayers with us every time, and kiss us even when we've acted bad."

Grandparents can also serve as official escorts to places such as the zoo, a museum, or the planetarium. (Many of these places now offer grandparent/grandchild memberships.) Spending the night with grandparents gives children a chance to experience visiting outside their own homes. One mother wrote:

> *"It was fun to let my children go to the grandparent's house on a regular basis. I wanted them to create some fond memories of going to grandparent's house. I remember that when I was young."*

One grandmother took each of her grandchildren on a special trip when he or she turned 10, and all the grandchildren waited anxiously for that magic birthday to arrive. Some grandparent friends of ours held an annual "Gramp Camp" where they invited all five of their grandchildren to spend a week with them (giving the parents a week to enjoy some good couple time too!). One year they all went to Disney World, one year it was the beach, one year they congregated at their home near Washington, DC, and went to see all the sites there. They even had matching t-shirts made that they wore on their outings proclaiming "Gramp Camp." One time, another couple saw them all with their t-shirts on and asked where Gramp Camp was, saying they would like to attend with their grandchildren the next year!

Here are some comments we received about good grandmothering mothers-in-law:

"I wish she lived closer (currently 7 hours away). We would love to have her nearby, our children adore her."

"I wish she could spend even more time with my children, she is a wonderful example for and to them."

"I love her investment in my children."

"I appreciate her family oriented values and the time she spends with her grandchildren. She always knows what is going on with them but is not overbearing at the same time."

"She is thoughtful and shows an interest in her grandchildren. She seeks to be actively involved in their lives."

"She smiles and enjoys the simple things of life, such as the way her grandchildren (my children) adore her."

Grandparents support the family

Another tremendously important role for the grandmothering mother-in-law is support of her children's marriage and the integrity of the family unit. One writer states that taking care of the parents actually makes grandchildren happier and more secure.[xii] This includes respect for their family boundaries as well as acceptance of the entire family into the mother-in-law's extended family. When asked how her mother-in-law had helped support her family, one daughter-in-law said:

"She has helped with my relationship with my children by supporting me and my decisions."

Others said:

"She has supported our decisions concerning our children (e.g. breast-feeding, home-schooling, and religious practices), even if she doesn't always agree with us."

"She values me, likes me, and values how I am raising her grandchildren."

"She has taught me to be the peace-maker in the family. Families will have stress and disagreements, but in the end we are very special and blessed to have one another."

"I appreciate her faith and understanding in raising children and the weariness that I often feel. She is uplifting."

"She has helped me see my role as mother and wife to be two very different but highly important roles."

What's in a name?

Back when I was calling all my friends to tell them I was going to be a first-time grandmother, it didn't take but a few calls before someone asked, "What's he or she going to call you?" That stopped me cold. I had no idea. I had called the only grandmother I knew (my mother's mother) "Grandmother" and my children had called my mother "Mama Frances", but neither one of those seemed to work for me (apart from my name not being Frances). But over the next 6 months my friends, co-workers, and family tossed around suggestions and we finally settled on "Gram." My daughter's mother-in-law didn't really care, but she settled on "Grandma." And so it came to be. If you're having trouble deciding on a name, http://www.banananana.com may have some you like. Some of the more common names in the U.S. include Nana, Grandma, Granny, Gran, Gram, Grammy.[xiii] A good source for names in other countries is http://www.namenerds.com/uucn/granny.html.

Whatever you choose, remember two things. First, the name might stick for the rest of your life so be sure it's something you want. And secondly, the name might change. One cute entry on the Name Nerds website tells the story of children renaming their grandparents because of who they look like (Alvin, of Alvin and the Chipmunks fame) and what happened to them (backing into a trashcan and having a butter wrapper stick to her butt, earning the name Butter-butt).[xiv]

Who makes the decision to have children?

The decision of whether to bring a new life into the world represents one of the most intensely intimate and personal decisions a couple will make.

And whose choice is that? Unquestionably it belongs only to the couple themselves. While a mother-in-law may long intensely for a grandchild, it is not her decision. One young woman, when asked what could improve her relationship with her mother-in-law said simply:

"If I didn't have to feel pressured to have children."

From www.CartoonStock.com, used with permission.

Some young women may also long for a child and end up feeling like a failure when pregnancy eludes them. Pressure in the form of jokes, unsolicited advice, or accusations not only makes them feel worse but can also build walls of hurt and resentment between mothers-in-law and daughters-in-law. If the couple make a choice to remain childless, then the mother-in-law must accept and respect that decision. She doesn't have to like it, but she must come to grips with the fact that that is a decision she is not in a role to make. To do otherwise could also damage the relationship with her adult child and child-in-law.

Divorce and grandchildren

One of the most frequently mentioned issues when dealing with divorce is the question of how that will affect the mother-in-law's relationship with the grandchildren. Some of the same issues may arise when an adult child dies and the son- or daughter-in-law remarries. In the next chapter we discuss this stormy sea and how to navigate its waters.

While grandparenting carries with it some of the greatest joys, it can also bring some of the greatest challenges. Clear communication (heavy on the listening part) with your adult child and child-in-law can alleviate misunderstandings down the road.

---

[i] Laura Rozakis, *The Complete Idiot's Guide to Dealing with In-Laws*, (New York, NY: Alpha Books, 1998), 233.
[ii] Gloria Call Horsley, *In-Laws: A Guide to Extended Family Therapy* (New York: John Wiley & Sons, 1996), 93-96 and Helen Q. Kivnick, *The Meaning of Grandparenthood* (Ann Arbor, MI: UMI Research Press, 1982), 98-105.
[iii] Horsley, 90.
[iv] Horsley, 79.
[v] Rozakis, 233.

[vi] Lucy Fischer, "Transitions in the Mother-Daughter Relationship", *Journal of Marriage and Family*, (Aug 1981): 613-622.

[vii] Evelyn Millis Duvall, *In-Laws: Pro and Con* (New York: Association Press, 1954), 142.

[viii] Ibid, 142.

[ix] Helene S. Arnstein, *Between Mothers-in-Law and Daughters-in-Law* (New York: Dodd, Mead & Co., 1985), 108.

[x] Ibid, 119.

[xi] http://jmm.aaa.net.au/articles/7796.htm, accessed on 11 May 2008.

[xii] Camille Russo with Michael Shain, *How to Be the Perfect Mother-in-Law* (Kansas City, MO: Andrews McMeel Publishing,1997), 118.

[xiii] www.banananana.com accessed on 16 Feb 2008.

[xiv] http://www.namenerds.com/uucn/granny.html accessed on 16 Feb 2008.

- 10 -

When the Marriage Relationship Ends: Divorce, Death, and the Mother-in-Law

Of the difficult life issues to come to terms with, divorce and death rank at the top. As one writer has so aptly put it, "Divorce shatters everyone's landscape."[i] The same could be said of the death of an adult child or child-in-law. While each of these events may bring differing emotions, almost everyone involved suffers from some form of grief, either experiencing it directly or helping with the family members who are grieving. Mothers-in-law may find themselves doing both. If the tragedy is divorce, she may still be doing all of the above while also navigating the stormy seas of anger, conflicting alliances, and legal wrangling. If the tragedy is the death of an adult child, she will be dealing with her own personal grief and at the same time helping to comfort her adult child-in-law, and often her grandchildren, who are all reeling from their own losses.

While acknowledging the important differences between divorce and death on in-law relationships, we have found there are some similarities too, especially the mother-in-law's concern about her continued contact and involvement with her grandchildren. Therefore, while we have divided this chapter into sections dealing with each, it may be helpful to read through both topics to find some insight into this maze of relationships.

Divorce

With divorce, all of a sudden, the legal and emotional attachments we've shared with one another suffer great upheaval and force all the relationships into chaos. How much chaos is determined by several factors, including the length of the marriage, whether or not children are involved, and the closeness of the relationship prior to the divorce.[ii] If the parents and parents-in-law live close to the couple or have frequent contact with them, they may have seen the trouble brewing for some time. (Or not.) If the couple lives in another state or have kept their troubles particularly quiet, the news of a divorce may come as quite of a shock. (Or not.)

Because divorce causes such a nuclear explosion in a family, including the extended family, if there is *any way* for the marriage to be put back together, it's worth it. I (Leanne) have seen MANY couples on the brink of divorce who, after deciding to give it one more try, went to counseling, rebuilt their marriages, and saved themselves and their families from that searing pain. Some couples claim they will get along better if they separate, but I have rarely seen that happen. It might happen in some galaxy far away, or many years after the sting of the divorce has healed. But if a couple can't work through issues when they are married, the chances that they can do it during the divorce process are greatly reduced. Also, research shows that children bear the pain of their parents' divorce through adulthood.

So, if you, the mother-in-law, have earned any influence with your adult child and child-in-law, talk with them about seeking counseling and working on their marriage. (Check out the "Resources" list at the back of the book.)

I have also known couples who decided not to rebuild their marriages and have gone on to divorce. While accepting that decision may be difficult for the mother and/or mother-in-law, she must realize that the decision rests with the couple alone. She may have influence, but she does not possess control of that situation. So what can a mother-in-law do? Here are some suggestions.

Emotional first aid for grandchildren
When the divorce process begins, emotions go into overdrive and even the best of parents can feel overwhelmed. Children, especially young children, can become confused and feel like their parents' crying and anger are their fault. In fact, even years after a divorce, many children carry a feeling of blame for causing their parents' divorce. "If I didn't yell and hit my brother, my Daddy would still live here," "My Mommy and Daddy got divorced because I'm a bad girl," and "I know [the divorce] is not my fault but I still feel guilty for yelling at my Dad the night he left home and never came back," are all statements made by children of divorce. Children can also revert to younger forms of behavior such as wanting to sleep with a long-forgotten teddy bear or clinging and crying. Others, including teens, may act out in ways they haven't before, such as having angry

outbursts or retreating and becoming withdrawn and quiet.

With so much turmoil occurring at the same time, and with one or both parents dealing with their own grief and loss, grandparents can step in to provide comfort and stability to grandchildren. Just listening to them and reassuring them that this is an adult problem that they did not cause can go a long way in shoring up a child's crumbling world. Encourage them to draw or write about their feelings and let them know it's OK to feel sad and even angry about what is happening.

But UNDER NO CIRCUMSTANCES talk badly to or about either parent. Remember, the child is part of each parent and calling his parent a name or saying he or she is a dirty rotten no-good lowlife can somehow work into a child's brain as, "If my father is a lowlife, then I'm half or more a lowlife too," and that will never do! Regardless of how you feel, put the child's feelings and well-being first. Many church and community organizations also offer classes and activities for children dealing with divorce, and if the child seems to be having prolonged problems sleeping, eating, or at school, it might be helpful to contact a counselor for the child to talk to.

Also, never put the child in the middle of a power struggle. Children are the innocents here and can carry lasting hurts from this type of confrontation. One 64-year old told us that even after almost 60 years, he can still remember his separating parents each having him by an arm playing tug of war with him while arguing over where he would go for the weekend. He said he still carries the pain of that moment because he loved them both and didn't want to hurt them. Avoid making the child choose in any way, even verbally, between his parents or his grandparents. Let your grandchildren know they are loved by you, by their other grandparents, and by both of their parents, and that you and they will get through this experience together.

How should I act towards my ex-child-in-law?

The days following the announcement of the marriage break-up until the final divorce can be a stormy and difficult time as everyone involved renegotiates relationships and their boundaries. Depending on the circumstances of the divorce, loyalties can be split along bloodlines, ideologies, or any number of other categories. It might be worth going back and re-reading the communication and conflict resolution chapters if you find yourself in these turbulent seas. You might also find counseling helpful at this time too, just to keep your wits about you. The divorce process may stretch your stress limits, lessen your sense of security, and push your patience to the breaking point, but remember that you are weathering a hurricane and when the seas calm again (as they eventually will), you don't want to look back in regret at something you did or said in anger or haste. How you weather this turbulent time may affect your future relationship with your adult child, your child-in-law, and with your grandchildren. Here are a few specific suggestions.

No bad-mouthing. Do not bad-mouth the ex-spouse, whether talking with your adult child or your child-in-law. As one writer observed, "What happens when your daughter makes up with her husband after you've told her you always hated the guy?"[iii] Or worse, what will your grandchildren feel like if you basically bash one of two people they love more than anyone? Here's a comment I received about some other complications of a mother-in-law's loose tongue:

> *"Bad-mouthing a mother-in-law or daughter-in-law only causes great rifts, usually between the spouses. I am divorced. One of [the] primary reasons is my mother-in-law. Now, that my ex-spouse is re-married, it has become even worse. After the divorce, I heard all the horrible rumors about how my mother-in-law*

did not want me to be married to her son. I suspected this all along. My children's step-mother has heard nothing but horrible things about me and continually tries to take over `mothering` my children. It is really awful."

Remember, that soon-to-be ex-child-in-law is the mother or father of your grandchildren. We need to help our grandchildren to honor their parents, even if we don't like them very much at the time.

Listen to both your adult child and to your child-in-law. Letting your child-in-law "vent" about your adult child can be hard, especially if you disagree with him or her. But whether it's your child or your child-in-law, listening and empathizing *helps to build and maintain relationships*, and, just because you listen and empathize, doesn't mean you agree.

Remain neutral as much as possible. The grandmother/mother-in-law should not take sides and lash out in anger against the other parent – remember, attacking a parent to a child makes the child feel bad. Also, remember that people tell the truth from their own perspectives. It doesn't mean they intentionally lie, but, especially during the adversarial process of a divorce, people often paint themselves in the best light and their spouse in the harshest light. The truth usually lies somewhere in between all the words. If you weren't there, take what you are told as *a* version of the story and not *the* story. Strive to take the high road and remind yourself often that it is up to your adult child and child-in-law to resolve their divorce issues, not you.

Keep in touch. Maintaining a relationship with both your child and child-in-law is important, especially for your grandchildren. Remember, women are the "kin keepers" of families. Generally, mothers-in-law and ex-daughters-in-law are more likely to keep in touch than mothers-in-law and ex-sons-in-law. In a 1987 study, daughters-in-law were more likely to maintain ties with ex-in-laws, particularly when they were the custodial parent of the in-laws' grandchild[iv]. In her 1954 study, Evelyn Duvall noted that many mothers-in-law and daughters-in-law still held a close relationship after the death or divorce of the son/husband.[v] Other studies also highlight this mother-in-law/ex-daughter-in-law bond.[vi] In one, 36% of the women maintained at least weekly contact with ex-daughters-in-law while only 9% maintained contact with an ex-son-in-law. Though we did not ask specifically about ex-in-law relationships in our survey, when we asked what was valued most about their mother-in-law, one daughter-in-law answered:

"Her values, as she stood beside me when my husband asked for divorce."

One factor in the quality of the mother-in-law/ex-child-in-law relationship could be the relationship they shared before the divorce. If they enjoyed a close relationship during the marriage, they have more potential to sustain a good relationship following the marriage. Several women I have spoken with over the past year have told me they think of their mothers-in-law more like their mothers and can sometimes share closer friendship-type relationships with their mother-in-law than with their mothers. If the mother-in-law and daughter-in-law are in the habit of sharing time together before the divorce, there's no reason for that to stop. Camille Russo even recommends the mother-in-law encourage other members of the family to continue contact with the ex-child-in-law, and suggests continuing holiday, birthday, and other celebrations with them; if that causes conflict with the adult child or with his or her new significant other, she suggests having the celebrations on a different day.[vii]

Many a divorced woman grieves the lost relationship when their mothers-in-law drop or reject them.[viii] While only 23% of our daughter-in-law survey participants said "My mother-in-law is more like a mother to me" (29% of the sons-in-law), a severing of those ties could sting quite badly, especially if the woman's mother has already died. Losing the relationship with her mother-in-law could be a hard loss for a daughter-in-law to bear especially under the weight of the other losses in her life in the aftermath of a divorce.

If you do decide to retain the relationship with your ex-child-in-law, don't think it will be just like it was before the break-up of the marriage. As people grieve losses, they go through the whole gamut of emotions, such as shock and denial, anger, and sadness before reaching resolution. Some of those emotions are likely to be directed towards your own adult child or maybe even towards you. Prepare yourself for that possibility. Just as in the early stage of your relationship, you, as the older and wiser woman, must "lead" in this dance insofar as you provide constancy and a good role model of behavior during this tumultuous time.

No "cut offs". As I mentioned in a previous chapter, a "cut-off" is when you make a decision not to have any further contact with a person. Cut-offs can create all kinds of long-term problems. If the person you cut off is the mother or father of your grandchildren, think about this: he or she could conceivably be the custodial parent of your grandchildren someday, especially in the event of your adult child's untimely death. A relationship cut-off could create a variety of issues regarding your continued contact and involvement with your grandchildren.

Another problem that arises is that one cut-off can breed another and another. I have dealt with many people who, instead of working through conflict with others, simply write them off. But resolving conflict actually helps us grow as humans and helps us in resolving future conflicts because we can use the lessons learned from the past. Continual cutting off truncates that growth, and often people who use cut-offs to avoid conflicts throughout their lives, find themselves as lonely elders.

And finally, relationship cut-offs seem to run in families, that is, from one generation to the next, probably through modeling. Children who cut off from their parents often have children who, in turn, cut off from them. In other words, cutting off is a bad example for our children and our grandchildren and we may set ourselves up to be the victim of a cut-off someday! Refer back to the communication and conflict resolution chapters for ideas on how to better handle conflicted relationships.

Replacement[ix]

When an adult child or former child-in-law remarries, the mother-in-law may find herself renegotiating relationships yet again. If she gains a new child-in-law, she may feel torn between her new child-in-law and her ex-child-in-law. Camille Russo offers such excellent advice, there's nothing to do but refer you to her book. As she says, "It doesn't have to be an either/or." And as she so aptly observes, we don't divide our love in half when we have more than one child, so why should we think we have to do that with our child-in-law? I know of many relationships where all the grandparents, parents and step-parents, siblings and step-siblings come together in support of a child's accomplishments and model tolerant – if not close – family unity. Keeping in touch with a former child-in-law can help your grandchildren feel part of a whole rather than torn between two families. Many times the former children-in-law themselves profit from strong mentoring relationships with their former in-laws.

However, issues of loyalty often rear their heads. A wise mother-in-law who chooses to keep in touch with both her current and former child-in-law would make it a rule to never share confidences or slight either in any way. In that way, she can better maintain both friendships. However, if those boundaries are not kept, a mother-in-law can expect conflicts to arise. Standing in this tension takes maturity and honesty both with herself and with the adult child and children-in-law involved.

The mother-in-law faces another challenging family situation when the child-in-law remarries and, in essence, "replaces" the mother-in-law's child with another spouse. This can happen both after divorce and after the death of an adult child. How does the mother-in-law then respond to the child-in-law's new spouse? Thankfully, I have the real-life example of my first husband's mother, who still refers to me as her "daughter-in-law" even now, 30+ years after my marriage to her son ended. I'll never forget the first time she met my husband, Ed, many years ago. She hugged him and said, "Welcome to the family!" At first, that sounded a bit awkward, but now that I'm a mother-in-law, I understand it much better and I respect her all the more for her acceptance and welcoming my husband into her extended family.

Keeping ties with your ex-child-in-law's family

When I think about my own relationship with both my son-in-law's and my daughter-in-law's families, I realize what a loss I would feel if we stopped seeing and communicating with each other. These are people with whom I share a common family, similar hopes and dreams for their futures, and so many other things. I often tell my son-in-law's mother that I love to visit her because we never tire of hearing about each other's grandchildren! To lose that sense of connection to another family can amplify the loss of the child-in-law. I'm thankful that my mother still keeps in touch with my ex-mother-in-law through cards and notes at birthdays and holidays. Even though their two children are no longer married, they share a grandchild (my daughter) and great grandchildren whom they both love very much.

Death

Death also brings chaos into a family. As the mother, you'll be dealing with your own loss of a child, someone who should have outlived you, taken care of you in your old age, etc. Clearly you'll feel the loss, as will everyone else in the family. All will be grieving while trying to redefine their roles in the family. While the grief may have a different nature from that felt during a divorce, many of the same issues will arise.

Emotional first aid for grandchildren

If you've been blessed with grandchildren, they'll likely need your support to deal with the death of their father or mother. Depending on their age and the circumstances of the death, you may still be faced with issues mentioned above related to divorce. For example, they may believe that if they had done something better or been a better child that their mother or father wouldn't have been taken from them. Or they may be upset that they didn't tell their parent that they loved them, or didn't get a chance to say goodbye properly. It's possible that you may be feeling some of the same things, and sharing that with them may give them a sense that what they're feeling is okay.

They may also be concerned about forgetting their parent. Now may be the time to introduce new traditions with the goal of celebrating their parent's life. Perhaps a yearly trip to the graveside to share their feelings, or a journal of what they would like to tell their parent. An important point for them to remember is that the parent will always be part of them because they have the same eyes, or the same nose, or the same sense of humor.

How should I act towards my child-in-law?

Attitudes toward the child-in-law are less of an issue than in a divorce. Because of the sudden absence of your child, both you and your child-in-law will be redefining roles. You may have shared information through your child, and will have to renegotiate how to do that. The child-in-law probably will turn to his or her own parents, since he or she has a long history of turning to them in times of pain. But he or she may also turn to you since you had a common bond.

Remember that there are five stages of grief, as defined by Dr. Elisabeth Kubler-Ross.[x] Each person who deals with death may go through phases of denial, anger, bargaining, and depression before finally accepting the death. It's possible that you won't be in the same stage of grief as your child-in-law. For example, your child-in-law may be complaining that their spouse was mean to leave them with all the housework AND the kids AND the need to work. This may mean that he or she is in the anger phase and is not criticizing but simply trying to come to terms with the death. Acknowledging that it is a process will help you work through the stages together.

Replacement

As with divorce, your child-in-law might, after a time, begin meeting new people and may even find someone that s/he wants to marry. This again is part of the process, when your child-in-law finally accepts the death of your child. One woman shared this story:

"I married the first time at age 20, to my high school sweetheart. I always loved and admired my in-laws because of their happy, Christian lifestyle. My husband and I were happily married for 19 years, when he suddenly died at age 40, leaving me with 3 children, ages 10, 13, and 16. My own parents had died many years before. The morning my husband died, his parents pulled me aside and told me that I would always belong to them and they would always be there for me. Eight years later, they are still here for me. They supported me in every way I needed. Then, when it seemed I was ready to think about getting out and meeting people, my mother-in-law told me that they encouraged me and would like to be considered as my parents and be kept abreast of what was going on in my life. When I met my current husband, they readily accepted and welcomed him. They even helped a lot with our wedding (they are in the flower business) and acted as my parents for our

wedding. They have basically adopted me as their daughter and accepted my husband as their son-in-law! They knew I had loved their son and they weren't afraid for me to move on. I will always love them for this. We are all very close now. I have been very blessed with two wonderful husbands and two wonderful, godly mothers-in-law."

While it's not your position to share your judgment about the new person (unless requested, but remember that they may end up marrying this person anyway, and negative comments may end up putting a future strain on your relationship), you may wish to communicate with your child-in-law about your role in his or her new life.

Divorce, death, and the mother-in-law

Some mothers-in-law find themselves in the middle of a mixed family, with both biological grandchildren and step-grandchildren. My husband grew up in such a home. His mother married a man with three sons. His step-brothers' maternal grandmother invited his step-brothers to visit her home often and she gave them money and gifts. But because my husband was not her biological grandchild, he was never invited to visit, given money or gifts, nor recognized in any way, and he felt the sting of that for many years. To the greatest extent possible, all grandchildren and step-grandchildren, especially those living in the same household, should be treated equitably. Remember, children are the innocents here.

As the mother-in-law, your role is vital to weathering both divorce and death. Resources are available (see the appendix) to help you maintain your sanity while also helping those around you.

---

[i] Laura Rozakis, *The Complete Idiot's Guide to Dealing with In-Laws*, (New York, NY: Alpha Books, 1998), 296.

[ii] Helene S. Arnstein, *Between Mothers-in-Law and Daughters-in-Law* (New York: Dodd, Mead & Co., 1985), 154.

[iii] Camille Russo with Michael Shain, *How to Be the Perfect Mother-in-Law* (Kansas City, MO: Andrews McMeel Publishing,1997), 153.

[iv] C. L. Johnson and B. Barer, "Marital instability and changing kinship networks of grandparents," *The Geronotologist*, 27 (3) 330-5.

[v] Evelyn Millis Duvall, *In-Laws: Pro and Con* (New York: Association Press, 1954).

[vi] Arnstein, 154 and Johnson and Barer, 330-5.

[vii] Russo, 154-57.

[viii] Arnstein, 155.

[ix] Johnson and Barer, 330-5.

[x] Elisabeth Kubler-Ross, *On Death and Dying* (New York: Scribner, 1997).

- 11 -

Cultural Matters: You Want Me to Do WHAT?

As we have indicated, there are a number of factors that make up the mother-in-law/child-in-law relationship. In doing this research, we thought that a source of differences in in-law relationships might be related to differences in culture and/or religion. According to the responses received, there may be a slight impact because of these differences; for those daughters-in-law with cultural backgrounds similar to their mothers-in-law, about 58% felt they had a positive relationship and about 59% felt they had a good mother-in-law. In contrast,

45% of those with different cultural backgrounds felt they had a positive relationship and 48% felt they had a good mother-in-law.

Although the impact may only be slight, it is still worth including a chapter about cultural differences and how to interact with in-laws from cultures other than your own. In addition to the information provided here, global business books (e.g., *Global Business Etiquette* by J. S. Martin and L. H. Chaney (2006)) or even the U.S. State Department website (http://www.state.gov/countries/) also have information about specific countries, as well as books written for modern-day educators (e.g., *Cultural Competence: A Primer for Educators* by J. V. Diller and J. Moule (2005) or *Racial Bias in the Classroom* by D. Leiding (2006)).

The information covered here relates to traditional elements of a culture; it is NOT meant to replace learning about your child-in-law as a unique individual, but can be used as a starting place to understand your child-in-law's background.

As is true when meeting any new person, first impressions are key. A great first step would be to become fluent in your child-in-law's language if it's not English. However, there still is no universal translator, and becoming fluent on your own may require several years that you simply don't have.

Learning a few words might be a good start. Key useful words and phrases might be "welcome," "hello," "thank you," and "please." A few are listed in table 12-1, and more can be found on various internet sites (such as babelfish.altavista.com, www.google.com/language_tools, www.ask.com, or http://www.elite.net/~runner/jennifers/), in library books, or even just browsing the language section of a book store. Perhaps asking your child to secretly help you learn how to greet your future child-in-law is an option as well. While you likely won't be as fluent as a native speaker, taking this step shows your child-in-law that you are interested in trying to connect with him or her and make them feel welcome.

A sincere smile of welcome upon meeting your child-in-law is almost universal, and may also be a good place to start your relationship with your child-in-law.[i] As mentioned in a previous chapter, non-verbal signals often say more than the words themselves, so anything beyond a smile should be used cautiously; non-verbal signals differ across countries just like actual languages. For example, nodding the head up and down means "yes" in the United States, Bulgaria, and Yugoslavia, as well as Turkey and Iran.[ii] In contrast, "yes" is shown in some parts of Greece by dropping the chin downward several times while jerking the head backwards abruptly means "no."

Table 12-1

Common Words and Phrases

Language	Welcome	Hello	Please	Thank you
Afrikaans	Welkom	Hallo	Asseblief	Dankie
Arabic	Merhaba	Salaam	Min fadlak/Min fadlik	Shukran
Chinese (Mandarin)	Huan yin	Nî hâo	Qing	Toa chie
German	Willkommen	Guten tag	Bitte	Danke
Hebrew (Israel)	Baruch haba/Brucha haba'a	Shalom	Bevakasha	Toda
Hindi (India)	Swaagatam	Namasté	Merker-bani seh	Shukriya
Japanese	Irashaimasu	Konnichi wa	Kudasai	Arigato
Portuguese	Bem-vindo	Olá	Por favor	Obrigada
Spanish	Bienvenidos	Hola	Por favor	Gracias
Swahili	Karibu	Jambo sana	Tafadhali	Asante
Tagalog	Mabuhay	Halo	Paki	Salamat

Hand gestures also vary by countries. The "thumbs-up" that is used often in the United States may mean "OK" or "I need a ride," but in other countries it may also mean "one" or even be a rude gesture. Imagine the horrors when you are trying to show approval but end up insulting your child-in-law! Even counting is done differently in different countries; in Japan, a single thumb is considered "five" while the thumb and index finger is "two" in Germany.

Oculesics is the study of eye contact, and is another thing to be aware of when interacting with different cultures. In the U.S., staring is considered rude, but in some cultures, maintaining eye contact indicates that you are paying attention to what the person is saying. In Asian and some Native American cultures, respect may be shown by not making any eye contact at all; when paying attention to someone, they may opt to look at the person's chin instead of their eyes. Misunderstanding why someone doesn't maintain eye contact with you as you expect can easily lead to confusion and upset.

Proximity (proxemics) and body contact (haptics) also play a role. In the U.S., the standard distance between people is 18 inches. However, in many areas of Europe, the standard distance is less, and some countries are more likely to kiss and hug when meeting new people. This can lead to an unintentional dance if someone from the U.S. is speaking to someone from Europe; the person from the U.S. may try to maintain the 18 inch "comfort zone" and back up to do so, which will lead the European to scoot closer to maintain his/her smaller comfort zone. Japanese and Southeast Asians actually prefer a greater comfort zone than those from the U S.

Another thing to remember is that different countries have different naming conventions. Some Asian cultures have the family name first to indicate the importance of family, followed by the personal name, which is exactly opposite of U.S. naming conventions. Some countries include both the mother's family name along with the father's family name, leading to confusion by some as to what the person's "last" name (by U.S. standards) actually is. Also, common practices in some countries are for women to keep their maiden name when they marry, potentially leading to more confusion. Find out early on from your child how your future child-in-law wants to be addressed and how to spell it.

How family members are addressed varies by country. In some cultures, a personal name is never used and family members are instead addressed by their title, such as "uncle" or "cousin." Sometimes, the family relationship is brought closer, and cousins are referred to as "brother" or "sister," perhaps confusing someone not familiar with the culture.

Another possible source of problems between cultures might relate to perceptions of time. For example, in some cultures, an arrival time is exact, and past, present, and future are distinctive times; a party that is supposed to start at 8pm actually starts at 8pm and so attendees should be there at that time or be considered late (and thereby rude). Other cultures see time as more fluid; an 8pm start time for a party is more of a guideline that you should not be at the party until after 8pm, perhaps as much as 2 hours later.

This perception of time impacts the pace of lives as well as family relations; in cultures where time is all connected, ancestors are key and family is often of utmost importance. Some cultures even include close friends or other social contacts as being of more importance than anything else (work, for example), and showing up late because you were talking to a close friend is actually expected. These cultures may be less focused on work for work's sake, and may focus on it as more of another social environment. Some cultures may take long (up to 2 hours), highly social lunch breaks. In other, more individualistic cultures, work is considered more important than family; work hours are adhered to and lunch is simply a time to grab food quickly so that you can return to working.

The contents of meals themselves vary between cultures and religions. Ham products may be considered unclean by some religions/cultures, while cows are sacred to others. Monkey brains are sometimes a delicacy while to others that may not be the case. Food options also may vary at different times of the year; some religions give up certain types of food in spring while others eat nothing during the day in fall. Try to get a sense from your child about your child-in-law's unique diet before serving up a large family dinner.

Meal times also differ by culture, and the time of the biggest meal differs. Some European cultures eat large meals later in the evening (e.g., 8pm) while other European cultures as well as some South American cultures have their largest meal in the middle of the day.

Cartoon copyrighted by Mark Parisi, printed with permission.

Not surprisingly, table manners differ too. Some countries in South America and Europe expect clean plates to avoid waste, while other countries expect food to be left on the plate as a sign of having had enough. Noise-making such as slurping and burping may accompany the meal to indicate enjoyment.

Not surprisingly, different cultures have differences in dating, marriage ceremonies, and family life, which you may have already encountered. There are three main types of dating in the world: marriage by capture, marriage by arrangement, and free-choice. Marriage by arrangement is the most common in the world;[iii] often the parents or a matchmaker determine the bride and groom for a number of reasons, including to maintain social status, to maintain fortunes, for political alliances, or because the couple are not considered worldly enough to know how to make a good match.[iv]

Wedding ceremonies differ; some are simple civil affairs and others are elaborate, multi-day celebrations. Many involve feasting in some form; in Turkey, the ceremony may basically consist of the feast, while in Germany, there often is a church ceremony followed by a feast. The bride and groom may be bound together by having their clothes tied together or with a ceremonial cord, they may stand together under a ceremonial canopy, or they may share their blood through ceremonial cuts on their hands.

Once the couple is married, there are two key issues that may color your interactions with your child-in-law: patriarchy, otherwise known as the family hierarchy (both age and gender), and patrilocality, or how close the new couple lives to the parents. In traditional patriarchal families, the oldest male is head of the family. Often, the hierarchy goes through the adult males by age and then through the adult females by age. Therefore, daughters-in-law are generally at the bottom of the hierarchy, so they are expected to support the family and do whatever the rest of the family desires. Since the mother may be directly above the daughter-in-law in the hierarchy, often the daughter-in-law is expected to do as her husband's mother orders.

In some cultures, the new couple lives with the husband's family, meaning they are patrilocal. Living closer has obvious advantages in terms of maintaining hierarchy as well as allowing the original family to support the new couple. Often there is more interaction among family members because of the co-location.

These two issues may impact how the mother-in-law is treated. In some cultures, it is disrespectful to be in the same room with the mother-in-law. For example, in Ghana, children-in-law have an "avoidance" relationship with their in-laws and do not eat meals at the same table with them. A Ghanaian friend of ours told us that when he married an

American woman from Memphis, he became known in her family as the man who liked cornbread. He said her parents would always invite him to share a meal with them, something with which he still felt uncomfortable. To try and entice him to the table, they would invite him to have some cornbread, which he said he would get and take into the other room to eat. To this day, they still talk about how much he likes cornbread.

Regardless of your religious or cultural differences, forging a relationship with your child-in-law is not impossible. Remember the importance of communication and learning about your child-in-law as a person, including what cultural and religious norms to which he or she adheres. And enjoy learning about another culture at the same time!

[i] J. S. Martin and L. H. Chaney, *Global Business Etiquette: A Guide to International Communication and Customs*, (Westport, CT: Praeger Publishers, 2006).

[ii] R. E. Axtell, *Gestures: The Do's and Taboos of Body Language Around the World*, (New York, NY: John Wiley & Sons, Inc., 1991).

[iii] B. B. Ingoldsby, Mate selection and marriage, in *Families in Multicultural Perspective*, ed. B. B. Ingoldsby and S. Smith (New York, NY: The Guilford Press, 1995), 143-160.

[iv] G. P. Monger, *Marriage Customs of the World: From Henna to Honeymoons*, (Santa Barbara, CA: ABC-CLIO, Inc., 2004).

- 12 -

Naomi and Ruth: A Model for In-Law Relationships

"Where you go I will go. . ." [i]

We often hear these words at weddings to symbolize the devotion associated with the joining of a man and a woman in marriage. A song based on those words is often sung at weddings.

But, wait! These words were originally used between two women, and not just *any* two women. These words were spoken by a daughter-in-law to a mother-in-law when the mother-in-law told the daughter-in-law that she (the daughter-in-law) did not have to stay and care for her (the mother-in-law). The loyalty and absolute devotion behind the words have been taken from the arena of in-law relationships into the arena of marriage. But relatively few in-law relationships today would elicit these emotions from either side. Because of that, a closer look at this relationship is warranted. Maybe we need to learn something here.

The story of Ruth and Naomi is one of the first recorded mother-in-law stories in history, so it seems very appropriate to include their story in a book about mothers-in-law. We'll see that Naomi, while engendering the love of her two daughters-in-law, was not perfect. Yet by working together, she and Ruth forged a close relationship that not only allowed them to survive, but also to thrive.

Naomi and her husband and sons lived in Judah during the time of the judges. Because of a famine, they moved to Moab where they had more promise of food. Eventually, Naomi's husband died, and her two sons married Moabite women. One was named Orpah and the other was Ruth. Soon, both of her sons died, leaving her with two daughters-in-law whom she would have considered foreigners. We don't know, but having daughters-in-law from another culture may have created some conflict between them. If so, we can only infer they were able to work through those difficulties.

In that culture, Naomi was actually worse off than the two young women, because they still had family and could return to their parents' homes. As a widow with no sons, Naomi faced a life of poverty and hardship. So, when she learned the famine in Judah was over, it was only natural that her thoughts would turn towards going home. With her immediate family gone, she longed for something familiar, something, at least a little comforting. So she set out from Moab bound for Judah, and, for reasons we are not told, her two daughters-in-law decided to join her.

At some point in the trip, possibly soon after they left Moab, Naomi told her daughters-in-law to return home to the house of their fathers where they could live until they found husbands. Orpah did just that, but Ruth stood firm and uttered those famous words,

> *"Don't urge me to leave you or to turn back from you. Where you go I will go, and where you stay I will stay. Your people will be my people and your God my God. Where you die I will die, and there I will be buried. May the Lord deal with me, be it ever so severely, if anything but death separates you and me."[ii]*

With that kind of unwavering devotion from a daughter-in-law, we might be tempted to think of Naomi as an almost perfect mother-in-law, right? Why else would her daughters-in-law want to leave their homes and go with her to a place where they had never lived, with people they had never known?

But Naomi was a real living person with very human hopes, dreams, and feelings, including a wide variety of emotions. (Sound like anyone you know?) In fact, a bit later in the story we learn that Naomi was in the midst of what today we would call a major pity party. We're told that when Naomi and Ruth came into town on their return to Judah and the women of the town welcomed her, Naomi told them to call her "depressed, bitter, sad, and lonely." Not very encouraging, but you get the picture. She could very well have felt that Ruth was another burden that she must bear. We just don't know. We also don't know what it was about Naomi that made Ruth want to stay with her.

What we do know, however, is that culturally, the two women needed each other. Naomi was unable to adequately care for herself because of her age and she needed Ruth to help her. In Judah, Ruth was considered an outsider, a foreigner, and she needed Naomi to help her understand the culture and customs of what was to her a foreign land. They seemed to have a common goal: survival. And we all know that working together toward a common goal can serve to bring people closer together. There is a definite lesson to be learned in that.

Ruth began working in the fields in order to provide food for both of them. She accepted the God of Naomi and lived by Naomi's cultural customs. When Ruth returned from the fields and showed Naomi all she had collected, Naomi began to see that something unusual was happening. Ruth was bringing home more than would have been expected from a day's work.

It turns out that Ruth was working in the field of Boaz, a distant relative of Naomi, and Naomi, recognizing the cultural cues, realized that Boaz had taken a liking to Ruth. Ruth did not know the customs of the culture, so she was totally dependent upon Naomi to tell her what was happening and what to do. Naomi saw where this relationship could lead. Can't you just imagine the gleam in the wise, old eyes of Naomi when, with Naomi's coaching, Ruth was able to attract and marry Boaz?

This story brings us full circle. Ruth and Naomi go from plenty to poverty to plenty again. When Ruth and Boaz have a son, they even bring the son to Naomi, who is called his grandmother.

We can learn several lessons from Naomi and Ruth's story. First, these two women encountered tragedy and famine and still managed to survive in a patriarchal society. Next, they formed a bond of friendship that enabled them to work and live on their own, something only men in that society would customarily be able to do. Most importantly, they were able to create opportunities that would have been unavailable to them if they were alone. Their closeness sparked their creativity and enabled them to not only survive, but also to thrive in a culture very unfriendly to widows and women.

Naomi was a mentor to Ruth, and Ruth listened. Family and cultural differences between the two women could have created all sorts of strife and hardship between them. But Naomi evidently communicated to Ruth in a way that encouraged Ruth, and Ruth listened and did what Naomi suggested to her. Naomi became a bridge to make it possible for Ruth to have her own husband and family. Mentoring can show us things we never realized we knew about being authentic women. Every mother-in-law needs to have this in the back of her mind; all of us can be mentors to younger women, including our daughters-in-law, and all of us can benefit from those relationships, just as Naomi and Ruth did.

So we have a wonderful story of two women. And we have a song that is based on their relationship. Put yourself in the place of either of these women and think about how you would have responded in similar situations. If you want to read the original story, it is found in the Book of Ruth in the *Bible*.

_____

[i] Ruth 1:16-17, *The Holy Bible,* NIV.
[ii] Ibid.

- 13 -

The 5-Minute Mother-in-Law: A Quick Reference for the Busy Woman

Years ago, Father Guido Sarducci of *Saturday Night Live* fame did a skit he called the "5 Minute University." His plan was to create a 5 Minute University because, according to him, that's about all college graduates remember five years after college!

Well, we hope you remember more than that from this book. But if you want a handy 5-minute refresher, or if you, like many of us, juggle family, work, household responsibilities, community and church activities, and all the other things you get called on to do, this chapter is for you.

Family Dynamics 101: A Family Factor Primer
- All families are different.
- People are different from each other based on many factors, including personality, the family in which they grew up, and the events a family experienced.
- Families change over time.
- When adult children marry, boundaries change.

Beginnings: Why First Meetings Are Important
- Children-in-law who said they liked their mothers-in-law from the beginning reported better long-term relationships with their mothers-in-law.
- Children-in-law may be different from you (personality-wise, religiously, culturally, etc.) and/or different than you imagined.
- Unrealistic expectations may hamper a good first meeting.
- Acceptance and respect form the key ingredients for successful first meetings.

- If you botched the first meeting with your child-in-law, humbly apologize and ask for a "do-over."
- Keep doing the right thing; keep trying.

The Wedding (War or Peace?)
- Women, in particular, each bring their ideas of the "perfect wedding" to the planning table; those ideas may differ sharply.
- Unrealistic expectations for a "perfect" wedding can spoil the day.
- Even if you are the one paying, use the opportunity to develop and practice good communication and conflict resolution skills.
- You are less likely to remember the color of the flowers or other such details than you are to remember feelings about that day.

Boundaries: Leaving and Cleaving and Other Boundary Issues
- "Respecting boundaries" represented one of the key issues from the children-in-law in our survey.
- As a new mother-in-law, you are:
  - o Stretching the boundary of the family to include a new person, and

- o Drawing and respecting the boundary line around the newly formed couple as a distinct, separate, and unique family unit.
- Your role is to teach, encourage, and mentor your adult child in the task of leaving your home and cleaving to his or her spouse.
- Boundary disputes can occur over money, demands on time, how decisions are made, where and how to spend the holidays, the running and cleanliness of the household, grandchildren, and unsolicited advice or criticism over these matters.
- Respect of boundaries begins with realizing you (the mother-in-law) are no longer in charge of that new family (your adult child and child-in-law), they are, for better or worse.
- Be thoughtful, respectful, and deliberate about what you say and how you say it if you want to maintain a good relationship.

Communication: Making Sweet the Words I May Have to Eat

- Listening is the most important part of communicating.

- Studies show we only hear about 50-75% of what is said to us; the rest of the time we make assumptions or we think about what we want to say. No wonder we have misunderstandings!
- You and your child-in-law are more likely to be able to discuss difficult topics calmly if you listen to one another and get to know one another.
- Many daughters-in-law said they would love for their mothers-in-law to call just to talk to them and get to know them as individuals.
- Heartfelt praise is a powerful way to build a better relationship. Notice your child-in-law doing something good and tell him/her about it!
- Unsolicited criticism (or even the perception of criticism) can be a curse to a good relationship.
- We need to receive at least 5 positive communications (praise) for every one negative communication (criticism) to keep our "emotional bank" solvent. How are you doing with your child-in-law? Adult child?

Conflict Resolution: Discord and Harmony

- Reasons for conflict include lifestyles, customs, and values; generational differences; personality differences; sibling and child-in-law rivalry; differences in working and non-working mother-in-law and daughter-in-law; overstepping the couple's marital boundaries by being meddlesome, possessive, jealous, or nagging; intruding (not respecting the couple's time or space by calling or visiting too often); child-rearing differences; and differences over household chores and management.

- Conflict avoidance, bottling it up, putting the spouse/adult child in the middle, screaming and yelling, and cutting off from any contact represent ways NOT to handle conflict.

- Effective conflict resolution involves listening to one another; treating one another respectfully (or choosing to treat the other person respectfully even if s/he is not treating you that way); and accepting the other person for who s/he is, not what you want him or her to be.

- Apologizing, forgiving, letting go of the hurt, and choosing to reconcile can help to heal broken relationships.

About Daughters-in-Law: Mothers-in-law Speak Out
- You and your daughter-in-law don't have to like each other, but you both need to accept each other and at least be able to be in the same room.
- Have a positive attitude or at least paste a smile on your face (which may, by itself, improve your attitude).
- Communicate with your daughter-in-law. If you want her to stop by or call "just because," let her know that. And then reward her in some way when she does.

Sons-in-Law: Those Generally Jolly Gentlemen
- Even though most of the jokes come from the male perspective, sons-in-law tend to be more predisposed to enjoy good relationships with their mothers-in-law.
- Sons-in-law relate some of the same issues with their mothers-in-law, but are more apt to handle conflicts with humor.
- The benefits of humor include improving health, building relationships, increasing creativity, and much more.

- Many mothers-in-law say their relationships with sons-in-law are more relaxed and less stressful than those with daughters-in-law.
- Treating your son-in-law respectfully may be more important than treating him lovingly.

The Grandmothering Mother-in-Law

- The decision to have children rests with the couple, not with the mother/mother-in-law.
- Discuss with both your child and child-in-law what your role will be both during and after the birth. (At the hospital? Visiting after the birth? How soon?)
- Often, a woman wants her own mother with her for the birth and immediately afterwards.
- Assume nothing. If you are going to assume anything, assume you will not be in the delivery room.
- If you go to help after the birth, help with the house (and older children) and leave the care of the baby to the parents.
- The birth of a child may mean re-negotiating boundaries.
- What do you want your grandchildren to call you?
- Never undermine the parents' discipline; you are the grandparent, not the parent.

- Follow the parents' rules when the children are in your care.
- Only step in if there is indication of abuse or neglect.
- Don't give your grandchild too much stuff; discuss gifts with their parents.
- Treat all grandchildren equitably.
- Grandparents can be a great source of love and support for children. Enjoy them. Enrich their lives.

When the Marriage Relationship Ends: Divorce, Death, and the Mother-in-Law

- If you have earned the right to influence your adult child and child-in-law, discuss with them the possibility of saving the marriage through counseling.
- The divorce, however, is the decision of the couple, not the mother-in-law, as difficult as that can be to accept.
- Remain neutral as much as possible.
- A grandmother can provide emotional first aid and stability for the grandchildren during the divorce process.
- Never bad-mouth either parent; the child is a part of that parent.

- Never put the child in the middle of having to choose who he or she loves.
- Keep in touch with your ex-child-in-law and his or her family for the sake of the grandchildren.
- Grandmothers can provide emotional first aid and support for grandchildren when a parent dies.
- When an adult child or child-in-law is "replaced" through remarriage of the surviving spouse, it will probably call for renegotiating relationships and boundaries in order to maintain relationships with the grandchildren. Patience and open, effective communication can help build these relationship bridges.

Cultural Matters: You Want Me To Do WHAT?
- Learn about your child-in-law's culture as much as possible, including the language (or at least some frequently used phrases).
- Ask your child-in-law about his/her culture; it can strengthen your relationship and you will learn not only about the culture but also about what s/he thinks of it.
- Don't make the mistake of assuming everyone from a certain culture is alike. Just as

Americans are different from one another, so it is with other cultures.
- Nothing takes the place of getting to know your child-in-law as an individual.
- Some cultural differences revolve around time (as in what is "on time" and what is "late"); hand gestures (some may be fine in the U.S. but considered crude in other cultures); proximity (how close or far you stand from one another); meals (types of foods or the times of the day meals are eaten); table manners; wedding customs; and where the couple is expected to live, just to name a few!

Naomi and Ruth: A Model for In-Law Relationships
- The story of Naomi and Ruth is one of the first recorded mother-in-law/daughter-in-law stories.
- Naomi and Ruth were from different cultures.
- Naomi was not a perfect mother-in-law; she was a real, live woman with all that entails.
- Naomi told both her daughters-in-law to go home, but Ruth refused. How did Naomi feel about that? We don't know.
- Naomi was "depressed, angry, and bitter" when she arrived in Judah.

- Naomi and Ruth were dependent on one another: Naomi knew the cultural customs and Ruth did not, while Ruth could work in the fields.
- Naomi was a mentor to Ruth, and Ruth listened.
- Naomi became a bridge to make it possible for Ruth to have her own husband and family; Naomi helped Ruth to secure a better life for both of them.

The End
or
The Beginning...

A Mother-in-Law & Daughter-in-Law Conversation Guide

Over the years, many writers have noted the most difficult in-law relationship often involves the mother-in-law and daughter-in-law. But it doesn't have to be that way!

We have designed a conversation guide that will help mothers-in-law and daughters-in-law learn to know one another better and develop their communication skills.

If you want to be a better mother-in-law and grow closer to your daughter-in-law, this guide is for you. Mothers-in-law and daughters-in-law who spend just one hour over the course of a few weeks or months learning and sharing through our Conversation Guide can build healthier and closer in-law relationships that impact the whole family.

You can work through the entire guide, or you can choose the conversations that best suit your family.

Best wishes on your journey together!

Conversation 1: My Family Tree

Before you meet:

❖ Take a few minutes and draw your family tree.

❖ Be sure to show yourself, your parents and all your grandparents. If you want to include brothers and sisters, aunts and uncles, cousins, that's OK too. It's your tree!

❖ Take a few minutes and reflect on your family tree and the questions on the next page.

Conversation 1: My Family Tree

Questions for Sharing:

❖ Share with each other the people and/or relationships in your family that influenced you the most. Why?

❖ Who did you enjoy spending time with? Why?

❖ What ethnic or cultural influences do you see in your family? Which ones played an important role in your life?

❖ What recurrent values, themes, or traits do you see in your family? Which ones do you want to keep, and which do you want to leave behind?

❖ Share a fond family memory and/or a funny family story.

❖ Share a family story that has been passed down from generation to generation.

❖ How do you think your family heritage shaped or molded you into the person you are now?

❖ What do you see about your individual families that are similar to one another? What is different?

Conversation 2: My Personality Preferences

Before you meet, consider the following questions:
(There are no right or wrong answers.)

❖ Do you feel energized by a roomful of people?
❖ Do you recharge your batteries with quiet alone time, such as reading a book, or just being with a few close friends?
❖ Do you enjoy spur-of-the-moment outings?
❖ Do you enjoy trips that are well planned and organized?
❖ Do you think you have pretty good intuition?
❖ Do you like to gather information or evidence before you make a judgment?
❖ Do you consider an issue from many different angles before you make a decision?
❖ Do you come to swift and sure conclusions?
❖ Do you make decisions primarily based on your emotions?
❖ Do you make decisions based primarily on your logic?

Personalities do not have to be alike for healthy relationships to occur. Different personality types make for an interesting and stimulating relationship. Honoring our differences helps us to accept another person for who she is, not who we want her to be.

Give your opinion:
Megan's 30th birthday was fast approaching. Her husband, Jason, knew she wouldn't want anything too elaborate, but he wasn't good at organizing things so he asked his mother, Pamela, to help. Pamela thought a 30th birthday was an important milestone and wanted to make the day extra special. She planned a party that would include inviting all of Megan's family, friends, and co-workers. Just before she called the caterer, Pamela called Megan and told her about her plans, thinking she would be excited. Megan was stunned and couldn't speak for several minutes. What can Pamela and Megan do?

Conversation 2: My Personality Preferences

Questions for Sharing

❖ Share your idea of a perfect day and how you would spend it. (Would your days be similar to or different from one another's?)

❖ Share some of your thoughts about the story on the previous page. What should they do?

❖ Have you ever been in a similar situation where someone misjudged what you might like or how you would respond? Have you ever been the one to misjudge someone else? If so, share some of that experience.

❖ How can you help others learn who you are, what you like, and how you feel?

❖ Share an area in which you would like to grow as a person.

❖ How are the two of you similar? How can your similarities be strengths in your relationship?

❖ How are the two of you different? How can your differences provide strength to your relationship?

Conversation 3: We Both Love the Same Man

Before you meet, consider:

❖ A mother and a daughter-in-law both see the same man from different vantage points.

❖ The mother looks at her son and remembers the child she loved, the hand she held, and the hurts she kissed away. She remembers his "firsts" and the way he changed and matured into the man he has become. Even though she sees a man in her son, she still remembers the little boy.

❖ The wife looks at the man whom she loves, full of strength and vigor. She remembers their first kiss, the day he asked her to marry him, and their plans for the future. She sees a provider, a lover, a friend, and the father of her children.

❖ You each play an important, though very different, role in the life of this man you both love.

Give your opinion:
Janet was planning to move into a smaller home and wanted her son, David, to help move. Unfortunately, when David agreed to help, he forgot that the day planned for the move was also the day he'd told his wife, Natalie, that he'd take the kids so that she could finally have a "Girls Day Out" with her friends, something she hadn't done since their second child was born. What should they do?

Conversation 3: We Both Love the Same Man

Questions for Sharing:

❖ Share a special memory you have about your son/husband.

❖ Tell a funny story about something he said or did. (Don't tell anything that would embarrass him, but something that he could also laugh about.)

❖ What special gifts, talents, or qualities does he have that you admire?

❖ What is his role in your mother-in-law/daughter-in-law relationship?

❖ Share your thoughts about the story on the previous page. What are some possible solutions?

❖ What is one way you can respect or honor his role in each of your lives?

❖ How can you honor him and/or show him that you value him in your lives?

❖ How can you encourage him to be the best he can be?

Conversation 4: The Wedding

Before you meet, consider:

❖ Weddings have long represented not just the uniting of two people, but a joining of families and sometimes even communities, tribes, and nations. While your family wedding may not influence world affairs, it represents an important milestone for the couple and for the entire family.

❖ The women of the family have often been thinking about their own and their children's weddings for many years. Unfortunately, they may all hold different mental images of what that "perfect" day may look like, which can cause conflict.

❖ Some couples are using the wedding planning to help them learn to negotiate and resolve conflicts between themselves and their families. Learning those skills early-on can help the couple and the parents negotiate future conflicts in a more effective and respectful way.

Give your opinion:
Carol had wanted a large wedding, but she and her husband had decided to elope and save the money for their education. Now that her son, Jason, is getting married, she wants to give him the kind of wedding she didn't have, a lavish affair. Jason knows that his fiancée, Yolanda, has plans for a small intimate wedding with just family and friends. So far, Jason has been content to not get involved. He told her that his mom never had the kind of wedding she had dreamed of and wants to be involved in the planning of their wedding. What should they do?

Conversation 4: The Wedding

Questions for Sharing

❖ Share a fond memory about your own wedding or a wedding you know about or attended and why it stands out for you.

❖ In what way can a wedding celebrate and honor the joining of two families?

❖ Discuss the story on the previous page. What are some ways they could resolve that situation?

❖ How can cultural influences or religious beliefs affect a wedding ceremony?

❖ How did/will you share in decisions about the wedding or wedding plans?

❖ What advice would each of you have for another mother-in-law or daughter-in-law about wedding planning?

❖ How have you respected one another's boundaries in making wedding plans/decisions?

Conversation 5: Communication 101

Before you meet, consider:

❖ We can't not communicate. In fact, even saying nothing can be saying something, depending on the situation. Over half of what we understand when someone speaks to us is what they show nonverbally through facial expressions, body language, etc.

❖ Listening definitely represents the most important part of communicating. But research tells us we only hear about 50-75% of what someone says. The rest of the time, we're thinking about what we're going to say or we go off on our own thought tangents. We can make a lot of incorrect assumptions when we do that because we don't get all of the information.

❖ We all have an "emotional bank account." It takes a minimum of about 5 positive statements or 5 statements of praise to make up for every 1 negative comment or criticism. When the ratio is less than 5 to 1, our emotional bank account may be "in the red."

❖ Sometimes, even when two people speak the same language, they might use words differently.

Give your opinion:
When Zoe was growing and up and asked her parents if she could do something, she might be told, "We'll see," when they actually meant "No." One day Zoe asked her mother-in-law Janine if she and her father-in-law would like to go with them to the beach for the weekend where they were renting a house. Janine, a busy lawyer, told Zoe, "We'll see." Zoe, thinking that meant, "no," invited another couple to the beach that weekend. When Janine called Zoe a few days later and said they would love to come and spend the weekend at the beach with them, Zoe was surprised and confused. What should Zoe and Janine do? What can they do to better communicate in the future?

Conversation 5: Communication 101

Questions for Sharing

❖ Discuss the story on the previous page. Have you had a similar experience where you and someone else used words differently? How did you handle that?

❖ Make a list of five things you appreciate about each other and why that is important to you (Ex: I appreciate that you are such a good cook because it reminds me of my mother's cooking.)

❖ Take turns sharing one item at a time from your lists and tell why that is important to you. Listen very carefully when the other person is talking and then repeat or paraphrase what she said (Such as "I heard you say you appreciate my good cooking because it reminds you of home. Is that right?")

❖ What do you think gets in the way of good communication?

❖ What helps you have better communication?

❖ How can we approach each other when we need to discuss something where we may differ?

Conversation 6: Conflict and Me

Before you meet, consider:

❖ What problems did your family face while you were
    growing up, and how were they handled? Were there crises
    or conflicts that you experienced growing up that brought
    your family closer together?

❖ How were arguments handled in your family growing up?
    How has that influenced you as an adult?

❖ What helps you to listen better when discussing a problem
    or difference with someone?

❖ How do you like to be approached if someone differs with
    you?

❖ What issues do you feel most passionately about?

❖ How do you handle anger? What helps you to calm down?

❖ Are you able to apologize and be willing to change?

❖ What makes it easier for you to forgive someone?

Give your opinion:

Maria was planning a baby shower for her sister-in-law, Jackie,
who was expecting twins. Jackie's mother (Maria's mother-in-
law) told Maria that since they didn't know the gender of the
babies, she had bought yellow plates, napkins, and other
decorations.   Maria   had   already   bought   pink   and   blue
decorations. What are some options for resolving this conflict?

Conversation 6: Conflict and Me

Questions for Sharing

❖ Look at the scenario on the previous page. What should they do?

❖ What do you think is the best way to resolve a problem with a friend? How difficult is that to do?

❖ What do you think is the worst thing a person could do when trying to resolve a conflict with a friend?

❖ Share a situation where you have had a conflict with someone and were able to resolve it successfully.

❖ Share a time when you forgave someone for something they did that hurt you. What is the hardest part of forgiving?

❖ Share a time when someone forgave you for something you did. What did it feel like to be forgiven?

Conversation 7: Celebrating the Holidays

Before you meet, consider:

❖ What important holidays or favorite traditions do you like to celebrate with your family?

❖ How have your celebrations with family changed over the years?

❖ What are your expectations for visits during the holidays?

❖ How do you feel about celebrating a holiday or other special occasion (birthday, etc.) a little earlier or a little later?

Give your opinion:

Mary is an only child and her family lives in the same town where Jake, Mary, and their 2 children live. Jake is from a large family, all who live about a 7-hour drive from them. Every year, Jake asks if they can go to his parent's house on Christmas Eve when his family celebrates by enjoying a big dinner, opening all the gifts, and attending a midnight mass. Mary's family usually has a quiet Christmas Eve; they watch TV specials together, and then go to bed early, saving all the gifts for Christmas morning. Mary and Jake have been going to her parents' house for both Christmas Eve and Christmas Day since they were married because Mary's mother says Jake's mother has other children but she doesn't. Any ideas?

Conversation 7: Celebrating the Holidays

Questions for Sharing

❖ Share a favorite holiday memory. What made it special?

❖ Share a funny holiday memory. Was it funny at the time? Or only later?

❖ What is one of the favorite gifts you have received? Have given?

❖ What do you like best about the holidays?

   o Fixing special meals
   o Searching for just the right gifts
   o Decorating the tree and the house
   o Going to parties
   o The music
   o Its religious significance
   o Sports
   o Family traditions

❖ If you had to give up one of the above elements of the holidays what would it be? What would be the hardest element to give up?

❖ Discuss the story on the previous page. What are some possible options?

❖ How could you work out conflicting family schedules to afford time together and allow for flexibility?

Conversation 8: Children and Grandchildren

Before you meet, consider:

❖ What are some of the values, traditions, and wisdom a grandmother should pass on to her grandchildren?

❖ What role should a grandmother play in their lives? How involved should she be?

❖ What are your expectations about gifts? Who should decide what is given?

Give your opinion:

Norma, a retired executive, travels much of the year to exotic destinations. When she comes to visit her son, Adam, and his family, she often buys several expensive gifts for the 8-year old twin boys. Adam and his wife Lisa are always happy to see Norma and they love her, but they live in a small house and the children's toys from Norma are taking over much of the square footage. Lisa has gently mentioned to Norma that she thinks the boys have enough to play with, but Norma just laughs and says she likes to spoil them. Lisa and Adam would like for her to spend more time with them and the boys because they enjoy her and enjoy hearing about her travels. What can they do?

Conversation 8: Children and Grandchildren

Questions for Sharing

❖ Share a favorite memory of a grandparent (if you didn't know your grandparents, share a story about someone else's grandparent or an elder friend). What was special about them?

❖ Who is the oldest person in your family that you can remember?   (Grandparent?   Great   uncle?   Great-grandparent?)

❖ Share your vision of what a grandparent should be.

❖ How would you like to be involved in the lives of your grandchildren? OR How would you like for your mother-in-law to be involved in the lives of your children?

❖ What values, traditions, and wisdom do you want to share/be shared with your grandchildren/children?

❖ Discuss the story on the previous page. What are some possible options?

❖ How can a mother-in-law and a daughter-in-law handle differences of opinion about the grandchildren/children?

Appendix A

Research Details

At the outset, we planned to create a survey to find out what works and what doesn't, according to mothers-in-law and children-in-law. The survey that follows includes key themes from multiple books and articles, principally falling into 5 key areas: Background, Characteristics, Family Characteristics, Pre-marriage Relationship, and Current Relationship. Also included are some solution-focused questions that let people say in their own words what worked and what didn't.

We also wanted to include personality questions since that is part of who we are. We selected questions from the International Personality Item Pool (IPIP; http://ipip.ori.org).[i] There are many personality characteristics on this site, but we narrowed it down to what we thought were pertinent characteristics. We used the entire set of questions for four personality scales, specifically:

- Adaptability[ii]
- Agreeableness[iii]
- Happiness[iv]
- Optimism[v]

Additionally, we selected specific questions from eight other scales. We decided to not use the entire scale for these characteristics because we thought the specific questions captured key elements we were interested in. Scales from which we selected questions include:

- Introversion[vi]
- Empathic concern[vii]
- Calmness[viii]
- Anxiety[ix]
- Cooperation[x]
- Perfectionism[xi]
- Traditionalism[xii]
- Trust[xiii]

We also wondered if having a sense of humor impacted how people perceived their in-law relationships. We included select questions from the Multidimensional Sense of Humor Scale.[xiv]

Respondents

There were 887 respondents who completed the survey; 30% were mothers-in-law, 63% were daughters-in-law, and 7% were sons-in-law. Ninety-eight mothers-in-law also answered as daughter-in-law.

Most respondents (92%) were white, with 4% Black/African-American and 1% Asian. Sixty-eight percent were Protestant Christian and 14% were Catholic; 8% indicated they had no religious preference. Fifty-five percent lived in suburban areas with the remainder evenly split between rural and urban areas. The majority (60%) had a bachelor's degree or higher.

Survey Publicity

Once the survey was created and available on-line, we created flyers that we handed out in the Memphis area and passed out at any conference we attended. In particular, we attended the Tennessee Association of Marriage and Family Therapy 2005 Annual Conference, the 9th Annual Smart Marriages Conference (2005), the 2005 American Association of Christian Counselors conference, the 2005 Pepperdine Lectureship, and the 2005 Lipscomb Lectures. We also advertised on-line, especially on Google.

We do know that the word got out beyond specific geographic locations, since we had replies from foreign countries such as Korea. However, this lack of diversity does leave the question open as to how "good" the findings really are. We certainly would have liked to have had more responses from a wider variety of people, but felt that the information we had received was a good start, and that we had sufficient information to find key themes that we could validate with other literature. If we had our druthers (and more money to better publicize), we would undoubtedly have gone to great lengths to capture that wider variety of respondents. Since we didn't have those options, consider this book a good start into the understanding of how to be a good mother-in-law.

---

[i] International Personality Item Pool (2001). A Scientific Collaboratory for the Development of Advanced Measures of Personality Traits and Other Individual Differences (http://ipip.ori.org/). Internet Web Site.

[ii] D.N. Jackson, S.V. Paunonen, & P.F. Tremblay, P.F. *Six Factor Personality Questionnaire Manual* (Port Huron, MI: Sigman Assessment Systems, 2000).

[iii] Ibid.

[iv] W.K.B. Hofstee, B. de Raad, and L.R. Godlberg, "Integration of the Big-Five and Circumplex approaches to trait structure," *Journal of Personality and Social Psychology* 63 (1992): 146-163.

[v] C.R. Cloninger, T.R. Przybect, D.M. Svrakic, & R.D. Wetzel, *The Temperament and Character Inventory (TCI): A guide to its development and use*, (St. Louis, MO: Center for Psychobiology of Personality, Washington University, 1994).

[vi] H.G. Gough, *CPI Manual: Third Edition*, (Palo Alto, CA: Consulting Psychologists Press, 1996).

[vii] K.A. Barchard, *Emotional and Social Intelligence: Examining its Place in the Nomological Network*, (Unpublished Doctoral

Appendix A

Dissertation: Department of Psychology; University of British Columbia; Vancouver, BC; Canada, 2001).

[viii] W.K.B. Hofstee, B. de Raad, & L.R. Godlberg, Integration of the Big-Five and Circumplex approaches to trait structure, *Journal of Personality and Social Psychology* 63 (1992), 146-163.

[ix] P.T. Costa, Jr., & R.R. McCrae, R.R., *Revised NEO Personality Inventory (NEO-PI-R) and NEO Five –Factor Inventory (NEO-FFI) professional manual*, (Odessa, FL: Psychological Assessment Resources, 1992).

[x] W.K.B. Hofstee, B. de Raad, & L.R. Godlberg, Integration of the Big-Five and circumplex approaches to trait structure, *Journal of Personality and Social Psychology* 63 (1992), 146-163.

[xi] Ibid.

[xii] D. N. Jackson, *Jackson Personality Inventory-Revised manual*, (Port Huron, MI: Sigma Assessment Systems, 1994).

[xiii] P.T. Costa, Jr., & R.R. McCrae, R.R., *Revised NEO Personality Inventory (NEO-PI-R) and NEO Five –Factor Inventory (NEO-FFI) professional manual*, (Odessa, FL: Psychological Assessment Resources, 1992).

[xiv] J.A. Thorson, I. Brdar, & F.C. Powell, Factor-analytic study of sense of humor in Croatia and the USA, *Psychological Reports 81* (1997), 971-977.

Good Mother-in-Law Survey

Thank you for your interest in our survey! There are 5 basic parts to the survey covering a wide variety of topics that we hope will lead us to find out what does and does not make a good mother-in-law.

The simple form of the survey should take about 20 minutes to complete. Your responses will not be sent to us until you click the final SUBMIT button.

We use some abbreviations throughout this survey:

- MIL = mother-in-law
- CIL = child-in-law
- DIL = daughter-in-law
- SIL = son-in-law

We have written our questions using present tense simply for ease in reading. If your MIL/SIL/DIL has passed away, we offer our condolences and hope that you will still complete the survey with them in mind.

Thank you in advance for your time!

Good Mother-in-Law Survey

Thank you for your interest in our survey! There are 5 parts to the survey covering a wide variety of topics that we hope will lead us to find out what does and does not make a good mother-in-law.

Section 1 - Background

How old are you?

_____

Are you currently:
- o Single
- o Married

How old were you when you were first married? (Leave blank if you've never been married.)

_____

Are you of Spanish, Hispanic, or Latino origin?
- o Yes
- o No

What is your race? (If you can mark multiple races below, please select the one race with which you most closely identify.)
- o American Indian or Alaska Native
- o Asian
- o Black or African-American
- o Native Hawaiian or other Pacific Islander
- o White
- o Other

What is your religion?
- o No religious preference
- o Catholic
- o Orthodox Christian (Greek, Russian, etc)
- o Protestant Christian (Baptist, Presbyterian, Lutheran, non-denominational, etc)
- o Mormon (Latter-day Saints)
- o Jewish
- o Muslim
- o Hindu
- o Buddhist
- o Other religion

How would you describe the city where you live?
- o Rural
- o Suburban
- o Urban

In what state do you live?

_____

What is the highest level of education you have received?
- o Less than high school completion, no diploma
- o High school diploma or equivalent
- o Some college but no degree
- o Associate's Degree
- o Bachelor's Degree
- o Master's Degree
- o Doctoral Degree

Which of the following best describes your job industry?
- o Not employed
- o Administrative support
- o Art (including design and entertainment)
- o Business/finance
- o Education (including teachers and librarians)
- o Food preparation/serving
- o Health
- o Legal
- o Management
- o Personal care/service
- o Sales
- o Science (including computers, engineering, mathematics, etc)
- o Social Services
- o Other

What is your household income?
- o Less than $25,000
- o $25,000 to $49,999
- o $50,000 to $75,000
- o $75,000 to $100,000
- o $100,000 to $125,000
- o Over $125,000

Are you answering this survey as a. . .
- o Mother-in-law (you will have the opportunity to answer later as a daughter-in-law)
- o Daughter-in-law **(continue with section 2, page)**
- o Son-in-law **(continue with section 2, page)**

Please enter the following information about your children: (Leave lines blank if you have less than 5 children)

	Age	Gender	Marital Status	Parental status
1st child	___	o Male o Female	o Not Married o Married	o Does not have children o Has children
2nd child	___	o Male o Female	o Not Married o Married	o Does not have children o Has children
3rd child	___	o Male o Female	o Not Married o Married	o Does not have children o Has children
4th child	___	o Male o Female	o Not Married o Married	o Does not have children o Has children
5th child	___	o Male o Female	o Not Married o Married	o Does not have children o Has children

I have additional children not listed above.
o Yes
o No

Section 2 - Characteristics

In this section are phrases describing people's behaviors. Please use the rating scale below to describe how accurately each statement describes you. Describe yourself as you generally are now, not as you wish to be in the future.

	Very Inaccurate	Moderately Inaccurate	Neither Inaccurate nor Accurate	Moderately Accurate	Very Accurate
I listen to my conscience.	0	0	0	0	0
I am concerned about others.	0	0	0	0	0
I feel little concern for others.	0	0	0	0	0
I am good at taking advice.	0	0	0	0	0
I adapt easily to new situations.	0	0	0	0	0
I can stand criticism.	0	0	0	0	0

How accurately does each statement describe you?

	Very Inaccurate	Moderately Inaccurate	Neither Inaccurate nor Accurate	Moderately Accurate	Very Accurate
I am a bad loser.	0	0	0	0	0
I want to have the last word.	0	0	0	0	0
I can't stand being contradicted.	0	0	0	0	0
I put down others' proposals.	0	0	0	0	0
I don't tolerate criticism.	0	0	0	0	0
I never give up hope.	0	0	0	0	0
I love life.	0	0	0	0	0
I work on improving myself.	0	0	0	0	0
I have laughed so hard that tears came to my eyes.	0	0	0	0	0
I know what I want.	0	0	0	0	0

How accurately does each statement describe you?	Very Inaccurate	Moderately Inaccurate	Inaccurate nor Accurate	Moderately Accurate	Very Accurate
I feel that my life lacks direction.	0	0	0	0	0
I am not sure where my life is going.	0	0	0	0	0
I am resigned to my fate.	0	0	0	0	0
I let others determine my choices.	0	0	0	0	0
I agree to anything.	0	0	0	0	0
I trust others.	0	0	0	0	0
I believe in human goodness.	0	0	0	0	0
I am wary of others.	0	0	0	0	0
I take things as they come.	0	0	0	0	0
I try to forgive and forget.	0	0	0	0	0
I accept people as they are.	0	0	0	0	0
I am inclined to forgive others.	0	0	0	0	0
I am not disturbed by events.	0	0	0	0	0
I tolerate a lot from others.	0	0	0	0	0
I get back at others.	0	0	0	0	0
I hold a grudge.	0	0	0	0	0
I am annoyed by others' mistakes.	0	0	0	0	0
I am easily offended.	0	0	0	0	0
I rarely get irritated.	0	0	0	0	0
I get angry easily.	0	0	0	0	0
I want everything to be "just right".	0	0	0	0	0

How accurately does each statement describe you?	Very Inaccurate	Moderately Inaccurate	Inaccurate nor Accurate	Moderately Accurate	Very Accurate
I seldom feel blue.	0	0	0	0	0
I feel comfortable with myself.	0	0	0	0	0
I adapt easily to new situations.	0	0	0	0	0
I look at the bright side of life.	0	0	0	0	0
I am sure of my ground.	0	0	0	0	0
I often feel blue.	0	0	0	0	0
I worry about things.	0	0	0	0	0
I feel threatened easily.	0	0	0	0	0
I dislike myself.	0	0	0	0	0
I am filled with doubts about things.	0	0	0	0	0
I don't mind being the center of attention.	0	0	0	0	0
I want to be in charge.	0	0	0	0	0
I tend to vote for conservative political candidates.	0	0	0	0	0
I tend to vote for liberal political candidates.	0	0	0	0	0
I worry about things.	0	0	0	0	0
I get stressed out easily.	0	0	0	0	0
I am relaxed most of the time.	0	0	0	0	0
Sometimes I think up jokes or funny stories.	0	0	0	0	0
People look to me to say amusing things.	0	0	0	0	0
Uses of humor help me to adapt to many situations.	0	0	0	0	0

How accurately does each statement describe you?	Very Inaccurate	Moderately Inaccurate	Inaccurate nor Accurate	Moderately Accurate	Very Accurate
Humor helps me cope.	0	0	0	0	0
Using humor is a great way of adapting.	0	0	0	0	0
Uses of wit or humor help master difficult situations.	0	0	0	0	0
Humor can diffuse an explosive situation.	0	0	0	0	0
I admire people who generate humor.	0	0	0	0	0
I generally have a happy outlook on life.	0	0	0	0	0
I have laughed so hard that tears came to my eyes.	0	0	0	0	0

Section 3 - Family History

How much do you agree or disagree with the following statements?	Strongly Agree	Agree	Neither Agree nor Disagree	Disagree	Strongly Disagree
My parents and I have a good relationship.	0	0	0	0	0
My parents and I enjoy spending time together.	0	0	0	0	0
I can count on my parents for emotional support.	0	0	0	0	0

How much do you agree or disagree with the following statements?	Strongly Agree	Agree	Neither Agree nor Disagree	Disagree	Strongly Disagree
I have a brother (at least one.)	0	0	0	0	0
I have a sister (at least one.)	0	0	0	0	0
My children and I have a good relationship. (Leave blank if you are a SIL/DIL)	0	0	0	0	0
My children and I enjoy spending time together. (Leave blank if you are a SIL/DIL)	0	0	0	0	0
My children know they can count on me for emotional support. (Leave blank if you are a SIL/DIL)	0	0	0	0	0
When I was growing up I heard negative things from my parents about their in-laws (Answer yes if you heard negative things even from just one parent).	0	0	0	0	0
My parents liked their in-laws.	0	0	0	0	0
My parents enjoyed spending time with their in-laws.	0	0	0	0	0
My parents received emotional support from their in-laws.	0	0	0	0	0
There is/was unresolved tension between my parents and their in-laws.	0	0	0	0	0

If you are a SIL/DIL, please skip to page 18.

Section 3 - Pre-marriage Relationship

Please answer the questions in this section about one child and the spouse of that child. You may answer about two additional children/spouses later in the survey.

How long has your son/daughter been married to his/her current spouse?
- o Less than 1 year
- o 1 year to less than 5 years
- o 5 years to less than 10 years
- o 10 years to less than 15 years
- o 15 years or more

How long did your son/daughter know his/her spouse before they were married?
- o Less than 6 months
- o 6 months to less than 1 year
- o 1 year to less than 2 years
- o 2 years to less than 3 years
- o 3 years to less than 4 years
- o 4 years to less than 5 years
- o 5 years or more

How long did you know your son's/daughter's spouse before they were married?
- o Did not know my son's/daughter's spouse before they were married
- o Less than 6 months
- o 6 months to less than 1 year
- o 1 year to less than 2 years
- o 2 years to less than 3 years
- o 3 years to less than 4 years
- o 4 years to less than 5 years
- o 5 years or more

How much do you agree or disagree with the following statements?	Strongly Agree	Agree	Neither Agree nor Disagree	Disagree	Strongly Disagree
My future son-in-law/daughter-in-law (SIL/DIL) and I immediately liked one another.	0	0	0	0	0
My future SIL/DIL and I enjoyed spending time together.	0	0	0	0	0
I tried to talk my son/daughter out of marrying his/her current spouse.	0	0	0	0	0
My future SIL/DIL welcomed my participation in planning the wedding.	0	0	0	0	0
My future SIL/DIL and I had conflicts over wedding plans.	0	0	0	0	0
My son/daughter often felt caught in the middle between my future SIL/DIL and me.	0	0	0	0	0
My relationship with my SIL/DIL changed for the better after the wedding.	0	0	0	0	0

Section 4 - Current Relationship

Please answer the questions in this section about the SAME child and SIL/DIL as in the previous section.

Is this your son's/daughter's first marriage?
- o Yes
- o No

Is this your DIL's/SIL's first marriage?
- o Yes
- o No

How much do you agree or disagree with the following statements?	Strongly Agree	Agree	Neither Agree nor Disagree	Disagree	Strongly Disagree
I have a good relationship with my SIL/DIL.	0	0	0	0	0
I enjoy spending time with my SIL/DIL.	0	0	0	0	0
My spouse and I provide emotional support to our adult children and their spouses.	0	0	0	0	0
There is tension in my relationship with my SIL/DIL.	0	0	0	0	0
I expect my son/daughter and their spouse to spend at least part of every holiday with me.	0	0	0	0	0
I approve of my son's/daughter's spouse.	0	0	0	0	0

How much do you agree or disagree with the following statements?	Strongly Agree	Agree	Neither Agree nor Disagree	Disagree	Strongly Disagree
My SIL/DIL and I are from different cultures/ethnic groups.	0	0	0	0	0
My SIL/DIL and I have similar religious beliefs.	0	0	0	0	0
My SIL/DIL gives me unsolicited advice and/or criticism	0	0	0	0	0
I give my SIL/DIL unsolicited advice and/or criticism	0	0	0	0	0
My SIL/DIL gives me unsolicited praise.	0	0	0	0	0
I give my SIL/DIL unsolicited praise.	0	0	0	0	0
I forget my SIL/DIL's name.	0	0	0	0	0
I love my SIL/DIL.	0	0	0	0	0
My SIL/DIL thinks I call or visit too frequently.	0	0	0	0	0
I respect the boundaries of my son's/daughter's marriage.	0	0	0	0	0
I have to manage my son's/daughter's house when I visit them.	0	0	0	0	0
My SIL/DIL apologizes when he/she is wrong.	0	0	0	0	0
I have a good relationship with my SIL's/DIL's parents.	0	0	0	0	0
I feel I have to compete with my SIL/DIL for my child's affection.	0	0	0	0	0

How much do you agree or disagree with the following statements?	Strongly Agree	Agree	Neither Agree nor Disagree	Disagree	Strongly Disagree
My SIL/DIL is willing to consider other opinions.	0	0	0	0	0
My SIL/DIL has a good sense of humor.	0	0	0	0	0
My SIL/DIL only tolerates me so I can visit with my son/daughter or grandchildren.	0	0	0	0	0
I enjoy doing things with alone with my SIL/DIL.	0	0	0	0	0
My SIL/DIL and I are alike in many ways.	0	0	0	0	0
I can discuss difficult problems with my SIL/DIL.	0	0	0	0	0
My SIL/DIL is more like another son/daughter to me.	0	0	0	0	0
I enjoy buying/making gifts for my SIL/DIL.	0	0	0	0	0
I think it is the SIL/DIL's responsibility to set the tone for the MIL/CIL relationship.	0	0	0	0	0
I can call on my SIL/DIL for her help without her keeping score of the things she has done for me/us.	0	0	0	0	0
I know my SIL/DIL would help if I needed him/her.	0	0	0	0	0
I can refuse my SIL/DIL's invitation without hurting feelings.	0	0	0	0	0

How much do you agree or disagree with the following statements?	Strongly Agree	Agree	Neither Agree nor Disagree	Disagree	Strongly Disagree
I am able to listen to my SIL's/DIL's opinion without feeling criticized.	0	0	0	0	0
I can forgive my SIL/DIL for past hurts and insults I may have received from him/her.	0	0	0	0	0
My SIL/DIL can depend on me to help if needed.	0	0	0	0	0
I can focus on the positives in my relationship with my SIL/DIL rather than the negatives.	0	0	0	0	0
I am a good mother-in-law.	0	0	0	0	0
I have a good SIL/DIL	0	0	0	0	0

Does your child have any children?

o Yes

o No **(Skip to section 5 on page 9)**

Survey-8

How much do you agree or disagree with the following statements?	Strongly Agree	Agree	Neither Agree nor Disagree	Disagree	Strongly Disagree
I support the way my SIL/DIL raises and disciplines my grandchildren.	0	0	0	0	0
I can refuse to babysit without hurting my SIL's/DIL's feelings	0	0	0	0	0
I enjoy babysitting for my grandchildren.	0	0	0	0	0

Section 5 - Solution-Focused Questions

Please answer the questions in this section about the SAME child and SIL/DIL as the previous section.

How are conflicts between you and your SIL/DIL resolved now?

When feeling the best about your SIL/DIL, what do you value most?

What is the single most important thing that your SIL/DIL has contributed to your life?

What single small change would have the biggest POSITIVE impact on your relationship with your SIL/DIL?

What single small change would have the biggest NEGATIVE impact on your relationship with your SIL/DIL?

The one thing my SIL/DIL does that I would like for him/her to stop is. . .

The one thing my SIL/DIL does that I wish he/she did more is. . .

You have just completed all sections for one child and his/her spouse. Would you like to answer about another child and spouse?
- o   Yes
- o   No **(Skip to last question on page 17)**

Section 3 - Pre-marriage Relationship - 2nd child

Please answer the questions in this section about one child and the spouse of that child.

How long has your son/daughter been married to his/her current spouse?
- o   Less than 1 year
- o   1 year to less than 5 years
- o   5 years to less than 10 years
- o   10 years to less than 15 years
- o   15 years or more

How long did your son/daughter know his/her spouse before they were married?
- o   Less than 6 months
- o   6 months to less than 1 year
- o   1 year to less than 2 years
- o   2 years to less than 3 years
- o   3 years to less than 4 years
- o   4 years to less than 5 years
- o   5 years or more

How long did you know your son's/daughter's spouse before they were married?
- o   Did not know my son's/daughter's spouse before they were married
- o   Less than 6 months
- o   6 months to less than 1 year
- o   1 year to less than 2 years
- o   2 years to less than 3 years
- o   3 years to less than 4 years
- o   4 years to less than 5 years
- o   5 years or more

How much do you agree or disagree with the following statements?	Strongly Agree	Agree	Neither Agree nor Disagree	Disagree	Strongly Disagree
My future son-in-law/ daughter-in-law (SIL/DIL) and I immediately liked one another.	0	0	0	0	0
My future SIL/DIL and I enjoyed spending time together.	0	0	0	0	0
I tried to talk my son/daughter out of marrying his/her current spouse.	0	0	0	0	0
My future SIL/DIL welcomed my participation in planning the wedding.	0	0	0	0	0
My future SIL/DIL and I had conflicts over wedding plans.	0	0	0	0	0
My son/daughter often felt caught in the middle between my future SIL/DIL and me.	0	0	0	0	0
My relationship with my SIL/DIL changed for the better after the wedding.	0	0	0	0	0

Section 4 - Current Relationship

Please answer the questions in this section about the SAME child and SIL/DIL as in the previous section.

Is this your son's/daughter's first marriage?
- o Yes
- o No

Is this your DIL's/SIL's first marriage?
- o Yes
- o No

How much do you agree or disagree with the following statements?	Strongly Agree	Agree	Neither Agree nor Disagree	Disagree	Strongly Disagree
I have a good relationship with my SIL/DIL.	0	0	0	0	0
I enjoy spending time with my SIL/DIL.	0	0	0	0	0
My spouse and I provide emotional support to our adult children and their spouses.	0	0	0	0	0
There is tension in my relationship with my SIL/DIL.	0	0	0	0	0
I expect my son/daughter and their spouse to spend at least part of every holiday with me.	0	0	0	0	0
I approve of my son's/daughter's spouse.	0	0	0	0	0

How much do you agree or disagree with the following statements?	Strongly Agree	Agree	Neither Agree nor Disagree	Disagree	Strongly Disagree
My SIL/DIL and I are from different cultures/ethnic groups.	0	0	0	0	0
My SIL/DIL and I have similar religious beliefs.	0	0	0	0	0
My SIL/DIL gives me unsolicited advice and/or criticism	0	0	0	0	0
I give my SIL/DIL unsolicited advice and/or criticism	0	0	0	0	0
My SIL/DIL gives me unsolicited praise.	0	0	0	0	0
I give my SIL/DIL unsolicited praise.	0	0	0	0	0
I forget my SIL/DIL's name.	0	0	0	0	0
I love my SIL/DIL.	0	0	0	0	0
My SIL/DIL thinks I call or visit too frequently.	0	0	0	0	0
I respect the boundaries of my son's/daughter's marriage.	0	0	0	0	0
I have to manage my son's/daughter's house when I visit them.	0	0	0	0	0
My SIL/DIL apologizes when he/she is wrong.	0	0	0	0	0
I have a good relationship with my SIL's/DIL's parents.	0	0	0	0	0
I feel I have to compete with my SIL/DIL for my child's affection.	0	0	0	0	0

How much do you agree or disagree with the following statements?	Strongly Agree	Agree	Neither Agree nor Disagree	Disagree	Strongly Disagree
My SIL/DIL is willing to consider other opinions.	0	0	0	0	0
My SIL/DIL has a good sense of humor.	0	0	0	0	0
My SIL/DIL only tolerates me so I can visit with my son/daughter or grandchildren.	0	0	0	0	0
I enjoy doing things with alone with my SIL/DIL.	0	0	0	0	0
My SIL/DIL and I are alike in many ways.	0	0	0	0	0
I can discuss difficult problems with my SIL/DIL.	0	0	0	0	0
My SIL/DIL is more like another son/daughter to me.	0	0	0	0	0
I enjoy buying/making gifts for my SIL/DIL.	0	0	0	0	0
I think it is the SIL/DIL's responsibility to set the tone for the MIL/CIL relationship.	0	0	0	0	0
I can call on my SIL/DIL for her help without her keeping score of the things she has done for me/us.	0	0	0	0	0
I know my SIL/DIL would help if I needed him/her.	0	0	0	0	0
I can refuse my SIL/DIL's invitation without hurting feelings.	0	0	0	0	0

How much do you agree or disagree with the following statements?	Strongly Agree	Agree	Neither Agree nor Disagree	Disagree	Strongly Disagree
I am able to listen to my SIL's/DIL's opinion without feeling criticized.	0	0	0	0	0
I can forgive my SIL/DIL for past hurts and insults I may have received from him/her.	0	0	0	0	0
My SIL/DIL can depend on me to help if needed.	0	0	0	0	0
I can focus on the positives in my relationship with my SIL/DIL rather than the negatives.	0	0	0	0	0
I am a good mother-in-law.	0	0	0	0	0
I have a good SIL/DIL	0	0	0	0	0

Does your child have any children?
o Yes
o No **(Skip to section 5 on page 13)**

How much do you agree or disagree with the following statements?	Strongly Agree	Agree	Neither Agree nor Disagree	Disagree	Strongly Disagree
I support the way my SIL/DIL raises and disciplines my grandchildren.	0	0	0	0	0
I can refuse to babysit without hurting my SIL's/DIL's feelings	0	0	0	0	0
I enjoy babysitting for my grandchildren.	0	0	0	0	0

Section 5 - Solution-Focused Questions

Please answer the questions in this section about the SAME child and SIL/DIL as the previous section.

How are conflicts between you and your SIL/DIL resolved now?

When feeling the best about your SIL/DIL, what do you value most?

What is the single most important thing that your SIL/DIL has contributed to your life?

What single small change would have the biggest POSITIVE impact on your relationship with your SIL/DIL?

What single small change would have the biggest NEGATIVE impact on your relationship with your SIL/DIL?

The one thing my SIL/DIL does that I would like for him/her to stop is. . .

The one thing my SIL/DIL does that I wish he/she did more is. . .

Would you like to answer about a third SIL/DIL?

o   Yes
o   No (Skip to last question on page 17)

Section 3 - Pre-marriage Relationship - 3rd child

Please answer the questions in this section about one child and the spouse of that child.

How long has your son/daughter been married to his/her current spouse?

- o Less than 1 year
- o 1 year to less than 5 years
- o 5 years to less than 10 years
- o 10 years to less than 15 years
- o 15 years or more

How long did your son/daughter know his/her spouse before they were married?

- o Less than 6 months
- o 6 months to less than 1 year
- o 1 year to less than 2 years
- o 2 years to less than 3 years
- o 3 years to less than 4 years
- o 4 years to less than 5 years
- o 5 years or more

How long did you know your son's/daughter's spouse before they were married?

- o Did not know my son's/daughter's spouse before they were married
- o Less than 6 months
- o 6 months to less than 1 year
- o 1 year to less than 2 years
- o 2 years to less than 3 years
- o 3 years to less than 4 years
- o 4 years to less than 5 years
- o 5 years or more

How much do you agree or disagree with the following statements?	Strongly Agree	Agree	Neither Agree nor Disagree	Disagree	Strongly Disagree
My future son-in-law/daughter-in-law (SIL/DIL) and I immediately liked one another.	0	0	0	0	0
My future SIL/DIL and I enjoyed spending time together.	0	0	0	0	0
I tried to talk my son/daughter out of marrying his/her current spouse.	0	0	0	0	0
My future SIL/DIL welcomed my participation in planning the wedding.	0	0	0	0	0
My future SIL/DIL and I had conflicts over wedding plans.	0	0	0	0	0
My son/daughter often felt caught in the middle between my future SIL/DIL and me.	0	0	0	0	0
My relationship with my SIL/DIL changed for the better after the wedding.	0	0	0	0	0

Section 4 - Current Relationship

Please answer the questions in this section about the SAME child and SIL/DIL as in the previous section.

Is this your son's/daughter's first marriage?
o Yes
o No

Is this your DIL's/SIL's first marriage?
o Yes
o No

How much do you agree or disagree with the following statements?	Strongly Agree	Agree	Neither Agree nor Disagree	Disagree	Strongly Disagree
I have a good relationship with my SIL/DIL.	0	0	0	0	0
I enjoy spending time with my SIL/DIL.	0	0	0	0	0
My spouse and I provide emotional support to our adult children and their spouses.	0	0	0	0	0
There is tension in my relationship with my SIL/DIL.	0	0	0	0	0
I expect my son/daughter and their spouse to spend at least part of every holiday with me.	0	0	0	0	0
I approve of my son's/daughter's spouse.	0	0	0	0	0

How much do you agree or disagree with the following statements?	Strongly Agree	Agree	Neither Agree nor Disagree	Disagree	Strongly Disagree
My SIL/DIL and I are from different cultures/ethnic groups.	0	0	0	0	0
My SIL/DIL and I have similar religious beliefs.	0	0	0	0	0
My SIL/DIL gives me unsolicited advice and/or criticism	0	0	0	0	0
I give my SIL/DIL unsolicited advice and/or criticism	0	0	0	0	0
My SIL/DIL gives me unsolicited praise.	0	0	0	0	0
I give my SIL/DIL unsolicited praise.	0	0	0	0	0
I forget my SIL/DIL's name.	0	0	0	0	0
I love my SIL/DIL.	0	0	0	0	0
My SIL/DIL thinks I call or visit too frequently.	0	0	0	0	0
I respect the boundaries of my son's/daughter's marriage.	0	0	0	0	0
I have to manage my son's/daughter's house when I visit them.	0	0	0	0	0
My SIL/DIL apologizes when he/she is wrong.	0	0	0	0	0
I have a good relationship with my SIL's/DIL's parents.	0	0	0	0	0
I feel I have to compete with my SIL/DIL for my child's affection.	0	0	0	0	0

How much do you agree or disagree with the following statements?	Strongly Agree	Agree	Neither Agree nor Disagree	Disagree	Strongly Disagree
My SIL/DIL is willing to consider other opinions.	0	0	0	0	0
My SIL/DIL has a good sense of humor.	0	0	0	0	0
My SIL/DIL only tolerates me so I can visit with my son/daughter or grandchildren.	0	0	0	0	0
I enjoy doing things with alone with my SIL/DIL.	0	0	0	0	0
My SIL/DIL and I are alike in many ways.	0	0	0	0	0
I can discuss difficult problems with my SIL/DIL.	0	0	0	0	0
My SIL/DIL is more like another son/daughter to me.	0	0	0	0	0
I enjoy buying/making gifts for my SIL/DIL.	0	0	0	0	0
I think it is the SIL/DIL's responsibility to set the tone for the MIL/CIL relationship.	0	0	0	0	0
I can call on my SIL/DIL for her help without her keeping score of the things she has done for me/us.	0	0	0	0	0
I know my SIL/DIL would help if I needed him/her.	0	0	0	0	0
I can refuse my SIL/DIL's invitation without hurting feelings.	0	0	0	0	0

How much do you agree or disagree with the following statements?	Strongly Agree	Agree	Neither Agree nor Disagree	Disagree	Strongly Disagree
I am able to listen to my SIL's/DIL's opinion without feeling criticized.	0	0	0	0	0
I can forgive my SIL/DIL for past hurts and insults I may have received from him/her.	0	0	0	0	0
My SIL/DIL can depend on me to help if needed.	0	0	0	0	0
I can focus on the positives in my relationship with my SIL/DIL rather than the negatives.	0	0	0	0	0
I am a good mother-in-law.	0	0	0	0	0
I have a good SIL/DIL	0	0	0	0	0

Does your child have any children?
- o Yes
- o No **(Skip to section 5 on page 17)**

How much do you agree or disagree with the following statements?	Strongly Agree	Agree	Neither Agree nor Disagree	Disagree	Strongly Disagree
I support the way my SIL/DIL raises and disciplines my grandchildren.	0	0	0	0	0
I can refuse to babysit without hurting my SIL's/DIL's feelings	0	0	0	0	0
I enjoy babysitting for my grandchildren.	0	0	0	0	0

Section 5 - Solution-Focused Questions

Please answer the questions in this section about the SAME child and SIL/DIL as the previous section.

How are conflicts between you and your SIL/DIL resolved now?

When feeling the best about your SIL/DIL, what do you value most?

What is the single most important thing that your SIL/DIL has contributed to your life?

What single small change would have the biggest POSITIVE impact on your relationship with your SIL/DIL?

What single small change would have the biggest NEGATIVE impact on your relationship with your SIL/DIL?

The one thing my SIL/DIL does that I would like for him/her to stop is. . .

The one thing my SIL/DIL does that I wish he/she did more is. . .

Would you like to answer about YOUR mother-in-law (MIL)?

o   Yes
o   No **(Skip to the last 3 questions on page 21)**

Section 3 - Pre-marriage Relationship

Please answer the questions in this section about your current spouse.

How long have you been married to your current spouse?
- o Less than 1 year
- o 1 year to less than 5 years
- o 5 years to less than 10 years
- o 10 years to less than 15 years
- o 15 years or more

How long did you know your current spouse before you were married?
- o Less than 6 months
- o 6 months to less than 1 year
- o 1 year to less than 2 years
- o 2 years to less than 3 years
- o 3 years to less than 4 years
- o 4 years to less than 5 years
- o 5 years or more

How long did you know your mother-in-law before the wedding?
- o Did not know my son's/daughter's spouse before they were married
- o Less than 6 months
- o 6 months to less than 1 year
- o 1 year to less than 2 years
- o 2 years to less than 3 years
- o 3 years to less than 4 years
- o 4 years to less than 5 years
- o 5 years or more

How much do you agree or disagree with the following statements?	Strongly Agree	Agree	Agree nor Disagree	Disagree	Strongly Disagree
My future mother-in-law (MIL) and I immediately liked one another.	0	0	0	0	0
My future MIL and I enjoyed spending time together.	0	0	0	0	0
I future MIL tried to talk my spouse out of marrying me.	0	0	0	0	0
I welcomed my future MIL's participation in planning my wedding.	0	0	0	0	0
My future MIL and I had conflicts over wedding plans.	0	0	0	0	0
My future spouse often felt caught in the middle between my future MIL and me.	0	0	0	0	0
My relationship with my MIL changed for the better after the wedding.	0	0	0	0	0

Section 4 - Current Relationship

Is this your first marriage?
- o Yes
- o No

Is this your spouse's first marriage?
- o Yes
- o No

How much do you agree or disagree with the following statements?	Strongly Agree	Agree	Neither Agree nor Disagree	Disagree	Strongly Disagree
I have a good relationship with my MIL.	0	0	0	0	0
I enjoy spending time with my MIL.	0	0	0	0	0
My spouse and I receive emotional support from my mother-in-law.	0	0	0	0	0
There is tension in my relationship with my MIL.	0	0	0	0	0
My MIL expects us to spend every holiday with them instead of my family.	0	0	0	0	0
I MIL approves of our marriage.	0	0	0	0	0
My MIL and I are from different cultures/ethnic groups.	0	0	0	0	0
My MIL and I have similar religious beliefs.	0	0	0	0	0
My MIL gives me unsolicited advice and/or criticism.	0	0	0	0	0
My MIL gives me unsolicited advice and/or criticism.	0	0	0	0	0
My MIL gives me unsolicited praise.	0	0	0	0	0
I give my MIL unsolicited praise.	0	0	0	0	0

How much do you agree or disagree with the following statements?	Strongly Agree	Agree	Neither Agree nor Disagree	Disagree	Strongly Disagree
My MIL forgets my name or gets it wrong.	0	0	0	0	0
I love my MIL.					
My MIL calls or visits too frequently.	0	0	0	0	0
My MIL respects the boundaries of our marriage.	0	0	0	0	0
My MIL "takes over" our house when she visits.	0	0	0	0	0
My MIL apologizes when she is wrong.	0	0	0	0	0
My MIL has a good relationship with my parents/family.	0	0	0	0	0
I feel I have to compete with my MIL for my spouse's affection.	0	0	0	0	0
My MIL is willing to consider other opinions.	0	0	0	0	0
My MIL has a good sense of humor.	0	0	0	0	0
My MIL only tolerates me so she can visit with my spouse or grandchildren.	0	0	0	0	0
I enjoy doing things with alone with my MIL.	0	0	0	0	0

How much do you agree or disagree with the following statements?	Strongly Agree	Agree	Neither Agree nor Disagree	Disagree	Strongly Disagree
My MIL and I are alike in many ways.	0	0	0	0	0
I can discuss difficult problems with my MIL.	0	0	0	0	0
My MIL is more like a mother to me.	0	0	0	0	0
I enjoy buying/making gifts for my MIL.	0	0	0	0	0
I think it is the MIL's responsibility to set the tone for the MIL/CIL relationship.	0	0	0	0	0
I can call on my MIL for her help without her keeping score of the things she has done for me/us.	0	0	0	0	0
I know my MIL would help if I needed her.	0	0	0	0	0
I can refuse my MIL's invitation without hurting feelings.	0	0	0	0	0
I am able to listen to my MIL's opinion without feeling criticized.	0	0	0	0	0
I can forgive my MIL for past hurts and insults I may have received from her.	0	0	0	0	0

How much do you agree or disagree with the following statements?	Strongly Agree	Agree	Neither Agree nor Disagree	Disagree	Strongly Disagree
My MIL can depend on me to help if needed.	0	0	0	0	0
I can focus on the positives in my relationship with my MIL rather than the negatives.	0	0	0	0	0
I think it is my responsibility to set the tone for the MIL/CIL relationship.	0	0	0	0	0
I am a good SIL/DIL.	0	0	0	0	0
I have a good mother-in-law.	0	0	0	0	0

Do you have any children with your current spouse?
o Yes
o No

Do you or your spouse have any children from previous marriages/relationships?
o Yes
o No

If you answered "NO" to both of the above questions, skip to section 5 on page 21.

How much do you agree or disagree with the following statements?	Strongly Agree	Agree	Disagree Neither Agree nor	Strongly Disagree
My MIL undermines our child-rearing and discipline of our children.	0	0	0	0	0
My MIL encourages our children to obey us.	0	0	0	0	0
I enjoy having my MIL babysit for my children.	0	0	0	0	0
I can ask my MIL to babysit.	0	0	0	0	0
I know my MIL will support me in my child-rearing efforts.	0	0	0	0	0

Section 5 - Solution-Focused Questions

How are conflicts between you and your MIL resolved now?

_____

When feeling the best about your MIL, what do you value most?

_____

What is the single most important thing that your MIL has contributed to your life?

_____

What single small change would have the biggest POSITIVE impact on your relationship with your MIL?

_____

What single small change would have the biggest NEGATIVE impact on your relationship with your MIL?

_____

The one thing my MIL does that I would like for her to stop is. . .

_____

The one thing my MIL does that I wish she did more is. . .

_____

When you think of a good MIL/CIL relationship, what is the one thing that stands out?

_____

What one suggestion would you make to others to improve the relationships between MILs and CILs?

_____

Please include your contact information below in case we have additional questions or would like to use your ideas in our book.

_____

THANK YOU FOR YOUR TIME AND INPUT!

Good Mother-in-Law Survey

Your answers have now been submitted to us.

THANK YOU FOR YOUR TIME AND INPUT!

You will now be returned to the main page.

Appendix B

Traits of a Good Mother-in-Law

Throughout their comments, our survey participants noted traits they appreciated, respected, and/or loved in their mothers-in-law. Here are the most frequently cited:

- Acceptance of others (especially those with whom she may not agree)
- Affection (warmth)
- Respect (of others, of boundaries)
- Faith (especially living their faith in actions and words)
- Kindness
- Encouragement (especially instead of giving criticism)
- Generosity (time, money, etc., both to children-in-law and to others)
- Financial Help (especially in times of need)
- Love of her children and grandchildren
- Friendship (especially with daughters-in-law)
- Humor/Cheerfulness

Appendix C

Resources

Counseling

American Association for Marriage and Family Therapy
http://www.aamft.org
112 South Alfred Street, Alexandria, VA 22314
Phone: (703) 838-9808 • Fax: (703) 838-9805
To locate a therapist near you:
http://www.therapistlocator.net/

American Association of Christian Counselors
http://www.aacc.net/
P.O. Box 739 Forest, VA 24551
Phone: (800) 526-8673• Fax: (434) 525-9480
To locate a Christian counselor:
http://www.aacc.net/resources/find-a-counselor/

National Association of Social Workers
http://www.socialworkers.org/
750 First Street, NE • Suite 700 • Washington, DC
20002-4241
Phone: (202) 408-8600

Navy Fleet and Family Support Centers
https://www.nffsp.org/skins/nffsp/home.aspx
Counseling information for Navy members and their families.

Helpful Websites

Smart Marriages - The Coalition for Marriage, Family and Couples Education (CMFCE), LLC
5310 Belt Rd. NW
Washington, DC 20015
Phone: (202) 362-3332   FAX: (202) 362-3332
www.smartmarriages.com
"Dedicated to making marriage education widely available and getting the information couples need out of the research labs and into their hands. We believe that people can "get smarter" about marriage, and that when they know better, they will do better."

Marriage Mentoring: 12 Conversations
http://www.12conversations.com
"We need to help couples grow great marriages from the start. Mentoring is a fun way to share what is ahead in marriage. Whether a couple is newlywed or entering a new stage of marriage, the 12 Conversations program is a simple, encouraging way to strengthen marriages."

The First Dance
http://www.thefirstdance.com/index.php
"Our mission is to help engaged couples manage the people stress of wedding planning and have more wisdom to carry over to their marriage."

Military One Source
Phone: (800) 342-9647
http://www.militaryonesource.com/skins/MOS/home.
aspx
Online and telephonic information and assistance for
military families on a variety of topics including
money, careers, elder care, child care, combat stress,
legal, moving, parenting, crisis, deployment,
education, and much more.

The HUMOR Project
480 Broadway, Suite 210
Saratoga Springs, NY 12866
Phone: (518)587-8770
http://www.humorproject.com
The HUMOR Project sponsors 52 international
humor conferences, HUMOResources mail-order/on-
line bookstore, and a Speakers Bureau that presents to
millions of people around the world.

Off the Mark Cartoons
http://www.offthemark.com/
"This daily cartoon appears in newspapers, on
products and inside a few bathroom stalls."
Just to tickle your funny bone.

Selected Bibliography

Arnstein, Helene S. *Between Mothers-in-Law & Daughters-in-Law: Achieving a Successful and Caring Relationship* (New York: Dodd Mead & Co), 1985.

Averick, Leah Shifrin. *Don't Call Me Mom* (Hollywood, FL: Lifetime Books), 1996.

Axtell, R.E. *Gestures: The Do's and Taboos of Body Language Around the World* (New York, NY: John Wiley & Sons, Inc.), 1991.

Barash, Susan Shapiro. *Mothers-in-Law and Daughters-in-Law: Love, Hate, Rivalry and Reconciliation* (Far Hills, NJ: New Horizon Press), 2001.

Bowdithc, Eden Unger and Aviva Samet. *The Daughter-in-Law's Survival Guide: Everything You Need to Know About Relating to Your Mother-In-Law* (Oakland, CA: New Harbinger Publications), 2002.

Chapman, Annie. *The Mother-in-Law Dance* (Eugene, OR: Harvest House), 2004.

Chapman, Gary. *The Five Love Languages: How to Express Heartfelt Commitment to Your Mate* (Chicago: Northfield Publishing), 2004.

Duvall, Evelyn Millis. *In-Laws: Pro and Con* (New York: Association Press), 1954.

Eggerichs, Emerson. *Love and Respect* (Nashville: Thomas Nelson), 2004.

Flatt, Bill, *Building a Healthy Family* (Nashville: Gospel Advocate Company), 1993.

Forward, Susan. *Toxic In-Laws: Loving Strategies for Protecting Your Marriage* (New York: Quill), 2000.

Horsley, Gloria Call. *The In-Law Survival Guide: How to Prevent and Solve In-Law Problems* (New York: John Wiley & Sons), 1996.

Horsley, Gloria Call. *The In-Law Survival Guide: How to Prevent and Solve In-Law Problems* (New York: John Wiley & Sons), 1997.

Kubler-Ross, Elisabeth. *On Death and Dying* (New York: Touchstone), 1997.

Leman, Kevin. *The New Birth Order Book* (Grand Rapids: Baker), 1998.

Markman, Howard J., Scott M. Stanley, and Susan L. Blumberg. *Fighting for Your Marriage* (San Francisco: Jossey-Bass), 2001.

Martin, J.S. & L.H. Chaney. *Global Business Etiquette: A Guide to International Communication and Customs* (Westport, CT: Praeger Publishers), 2006.

Monger, G.P. *Marriage Customs of the World: From Henna to Honeymoons* (Santa Barbara, CA: ABC-CLIO, Inc.), 2004.

Morris, Joseph. *The Mother-in-Law Daughter-in-Law Conflict: The Exploration and Improvement of the Mother-in-Law – Daughter-in-Law Relationship* (1st Books), 2004.

Rozakis, Laurie E. *The Complete Idiot's Guide to Dealing with In-Laws* (New York: Alpha Books), 1998.

Russo, Camille. *How to Be the Perfect Mother-in-Law* (Kansas City, MO: Andrews McMeel Publishing), 1997.

Silverman, Ilena. *I Married My Mother-in-Law: And Other Tales of In-Laws We Can't Live With or Can't Live Without* (New York: Riverhead Books), 2006.

Worthington, Everett L. *Forgiveness and Reconciliation: Theory and Application* (New York: Taylor & Francis), 2006.

Worthington, Everett L. *The Power of Forgiving* (West Conshohocken, PA: Templeton Foundation Press), 2005.